Short Role-playing Simulations for US History Classrooms

by Richard Di Giacomo

ISBN 0-9706237-1-2

043905

Acknowledgements

I would like to dedicate this book to Donald Gregory of Gregory Publications for encouraging me to someday publish books of my own. I would like to thank Diane Hart for all of her helpful suggestions for revisions and for helping me to market this book. I would also like to thank Aaron Willis and others at Social Studies School Service for helping me to first get the book distributed to the educational market, and Nina Linebaugh and others at Teacher's Discovery for their enthusiastic support for my books. Special thanks go to Ian Croxall of warflag.com for permission to use some of his beautifully- drawn flags in this book. Thanks also go to Rob Raeside, Director of Flags of the World at http://flagspot.net/flags/ for use of the Russian Imperial flag. Finally, I would like to thank the students of Yerba Buena High School in San Jose, California and Henry M. Gunn High School in Palo Alto, California for play-testing these games. Without their patient suggestions for improvements and clarifications this book would not have been possible.

Table of Contents

Simulation Title	National Standards Number	Description
Reconstruction Simulation	Era 5 Standard 3	How various reconstruction plans succeeded or failed
Taking Colonies	Era 6 Standard 4B	Roots and development of American expansionism
Great Powers Game	Era 7: 2B	The causes of World War I and why the United States intervened
Strike Simulation	Era 6: 1A Standard 3B	Analyze the causes and effects of escalating labor conflict.
W.W.II Debates	Era 8: 3C	Analyze the effects of World War II
Cold War Simulation	Era 9 Standard 2A, 2B	American foreign policy during the Cold War nuclear politics, containment policy
Cuban Missile Crisis Simulation	Era 9 Standard 2A, 2B	American foreign policy during the Cold War nuclear politics, containment policy
Hippie Day	Era 9 Standard 2C Standard 4A, 4B	How the (Vietnam) War continued to affect postwar politics and culture The struggle for racial and gender equality
20th Century Slang	Eras 7-9 Several standards	Meets several standards that deal with the impact of events on society or social change
US History Counterfactuals	All eras	"What if...?" questions covering all eras of US History

Introduction

This book is an exciting collection of role-playing simulations for Social Studies classrooms. Although most of the simulations are written for World and US History, some of them would work equally as well in Economics or Government classes. All of these simulations have been play tested in classes ranging from Junior High to High School and at ability levels ranging from sheltered classes to honors.

What is a role-playing simulation?

Role-playing simulations attempt to put the student in the position of a person in a particular time and place. All of the simulations involve group problem solving and conflict resolution. The students are given a character sheet, which describes the groups needs and desires, a brief description of the historical problem and a copy of the rules of the game. Familiarity with fantasy role playing games is a plus, but certainly not required. The individual assumes the role they choose and makes decisions as the character would make during that particular time period. No pre-set limits are placed on a particular person's choices as long as they are within the realm of what was historically possible. Because of the freedom to choose in these games the outcome is very unpredictable. No two classes finish the simulation in the exact same way which leads to some very interesting classroom discussions about why things turned out the way they did, what could have happened differently, and how the simulation compares to what actually occurred in history.

How are these activities different from other simulations?

Unlike many simulations that are commercially available, these games can usually be played in one or two class periods. Their open-ended nature allows for playing up to one week if time permits, but after a couple of days you will find that most of the possibilities have been exhausted and continued play will have only limited instructional value. Another key advantage to this system is the cost. Everything you need to play these simulations can be reproduced out of this book. There are no tiresome charts to deal with and minimal set up and cleanup time required allowing for maximum role-playing time. As much as possible, pieces have been kept to a minimum to make cleanup and storage easier and to keep costs down for teachers on a budget. The emphasis is on role-playing so that the student can get as much as possible out of their personal learning experience and not get tied up in the mechanics of a complicated rules system.

How are the simulations used?

The best way to use these simulations is at the beginning of a unit when students have little prior knowledge of the historical outcome of a particular conflict. This allows a clean slate for actions instead of a predictable imitation of history just because "That's the way it had to be". When the teacher does begin the regular instructional part of the unit, the students will automatically make comments like, "Wow! That is just like what happened in the game" or "Now I understand why they did what they did". We all know that students remember better what they do than what they heard or read about, so these simulations allow for an unforgettable experience, which will bring history alive for them.

After the simulation is completed the teacher can lead a very interesting discussion of why things happened the way they did and how they might have turned out differently in the game or actually did turn out differently in other countries. This debriefing period is the most valuable portion of the activity. Students will be eager to participate because they were active stakeholders in the decisions made instead of passive listeners hearing about other people's problems from long ago. The activities build historical understanding, empathy for the viewpoints of others and group decision-making skills.

Follow up activities might include an essay comparing the game to what actually occurred in history or a visit to the internet newsgroup on alternative history where the students' questions can be bounced off a group of history professors, students and aficionados across the world. This can be a very valuable form of feed back. The simulations can also be used at the end of a unit for a form of alternative assessment to see how well they can apply the skills they have learned to an actual historical problem.

What do students have to say about these simulations?

Invariably students rate these activities among their favorite activities of the year. Returning students have stated that they are the things they best remember about the class years later. Under motivated students will often flourish in these activities because they have found a place were their abilities can shine. Gifted students enjoy the challenge of adding as much realism and detail to the activity as possible and often enjoy taking a leadership role in the bargaining.

Many students have commented to me that "This is the first time I have ever been interested in a history class" or "This makes me feel like I was really there because it was so exciting". Often discussion over what has occurred will pour over into other classes, lunch time or after school. Students will compare what happened to their friends' classes and eagerly return the next day to see if the outcome is as they expected.

How did this book come to be?

The author has played role-playing games since he was a teenager himself. The fun and unpredictability of the outcome of a given situation got him thinking about how history might have been different. As a lover of history and a player of every kind of game from checkers to fantasy role-playing and historical miniature battles it was a natural step from tinkering with rules to developing his own games. He has experimented with these games from his first year of teaching, improving upon them every year based upon feedback from students. As he began to share these simulations with colleagues, they unanimously urged him to publish them to make them available for other teachers.

Reconstruction Simulation Teacher's Guide:

Objective: To appreciate the complexity of issues that the nation faced in its attempt to reunify and rebuild after the Civil War. To have empathy for those who had to make difficult decisions about changing race relations, social structure and civil rights.

Duration: 1-2 class periods.

Materials: Run off enough copies of the simulation description for everyone and enough of the group problems for each group. Answers can be recorded on a separate sheet of paper. Just have the students label the group and identify its members.

Procedure:
1. Divide up the class into the four social groups.
2. Conduct negotiating and discussion according to the rules on the student handout.
3. Stop the simulation and collect the written responses from each group.
4. Conduct the debriefing.
5. Evaluate students' responses based on completeness and understanding of the issues.

Teacher Recommendations:
1. This simulation involves more discussion than bargaining. Consensus need not be reached because in reality not all members of a social class would react to a given problem in the same way.

2. Actively monitor students' discussion to see that they are not introducing anachronisms like welfare or federal income taxes into the 1860's.

3. Stress to students the importance of thinking as people would have thought in the late 1860's. Tell them not to insert their own modern ideas of what is right. They must be faithful to the role they are playing, even if they disagree with the views of the group they are representing.

4. Review students' written responses before they turn them in. Check for inaccuracies and incompleteness. When grading take off points for anything incomplete or not fully explained.

Debriefing: read each group's plan aloud and discuss the following:

1. How realistic is this plan? Which aspects would work and which ones would not?

2. Was anyone a part of a group that felt differently than how they feel personally about these issues? How did it feel playing the role of someone different than you?

3. Knowing what you do now, why do suppose these groups reacted to these challenges as they did? What does it tell you about the difficulty of and resistance to reform? Do some of these problems still have ramifications today?

4. Was there anyone who disagreed with the majority of your group? Do you suppose that happened in real life? Why do different people react to the same challenges differently? What effect do you think that his had on party politics in the years after the Civil War?

Reconstruction Simulation:

Overall goals: to reconstruct the nation which has been torn apart by the Civil War. The groups that we will represent are:

A) Radical Republicans: The victorious northerners of the Republican Party who want to make radical reforms to punish the South and guarantee the rights of the newly freed slaves.

B) Defeated Southern Leaders: The war has been lost and the north has freed the slaves. They had to decide whether to heal old wounds or fight for what was lost.

C) Freedmen: Former slaves who now must find work and find their place in politics, the economy and society.

D) Moderate Republicans: Leaders like President Lincoln and Vice President Johnson who wish to take it easy on the South so that they will peacefully rejoin the Union without too much resentment.

How the game is played: Form groups of from 2-8 members. Read the overall goals for your group. Then begin reading the individual problems that your group must face. Discuss solutions to these problems openly. Record your responses on a separate sheet of paper. If members of your group disagree upon a particular solution record both responses and indicate that some will do one thing and some will do another. You are representing a whole class of society, so not everyone will respond to challenges in the same way.
Please keep in mind that you must be as specific as possible in your proposed solutions. For example, it is not enough just to say, "We will create schools to educate Freed Blacks". Which level of government will do this, local, state or Federal? Who will pay for it? Keep in mind the time period that you are dealing with. There are no income taxes, the Federal Government is relatively small and not used to dealing directly with social problems. There are no civil rights laws dealing with race or gender. Only white males with property can vote, for example. There are no government agencies that give financial aid to minorities of any kind.
Most importantly: try to think as people would have thought in the late 1860's. Don't try and insert your own modern ideas of what is right. Be faithful to the role you are playing even if you disagree with the views of the group you are representing.

Group roles: Each group will need at least one of the following. Small groups may cover more than one role:

Facilitator: Leads the discussion and makes sure everyone has a chance to participate

Recorder: Writes down the final responses to the questions. Clearly label which question is being addressed and check for completeness, spelling and grammar errors.

Compromiser: Tries to come to an agreement with which everyone can live.

Group A: Radical Republicans

You have won the war and are proud of it. You intend to have the Republican Party take credit for saving the Union, and never let anybody forget it. You are not beyond waving a bloody shirt during political speeches to remind people what the Confederacy did to this country. You believe in severely punishing the South for breaking away from the Union and starting the war. You are glad that the question of whether the federal government should be more powerful than the states has been settled once and for all in favor of the federal government. You are anxious to use that new power to show the defeated southern states who is boss. You feel that if the South is treated too lightly they might rise up in rebellion again, and one civil war was enough. You are beginning to lose patience with the President for being too soft on the South and not moving quickly enough to help free blacks obtain their political and economic rights. Here are the problems you must discuss and solve together:

1. How will you treat the leaders of the old Confederate government? Some of them would like to run for office and rejoin your government.

2. How will you deal with the Confederate prisoners of war? How and when will you release them? Should they be punished for fighting against the United States? The usual punishment for treason is the death penalty. Does everyone get this, officers and enlisted men alike?

3. What do you do with the occupied areas of the South? What rules do you make for states that want to rejoin the Union? How do people get back their citizenship in the Union?

4. How will you guarantee the rights of free blacks? Many southerners are still very prejudiced against blacks and do not want to give them their rights. They want to bring back the old way of life before slavery was abolished. How do you educate the blacks and teach them job skills? Most of them only knew farming before they got their freedom, how can they farm if they don't own land? You would like to have blacks vote and participate in government like other men, but how can they vote and run for office if most can't read and don't have any political experience?

Group B: Defeated Southern Leaders

Despite your best efforts you have lost the war. Outnumbered by the North, and unable to get the support from England or France that you needed, your under supplied troops were forced to surrender to the North unconditionally. The Union government has occupied your land, freed the slaves, and dissolved the Confederate Government. The lifestyle that you were used to in slavery times will never be again; it is now "gone with the wind". How do you live in peace with the former slaves now that the North is forcing you to share power with them? How can you try to regain your wealth now that the war has destroyed your lands and property, and the freed slaves insist that you pay them for their work? How do you make peace with the North and rejoin the Union you fought so hard to break away from? Here are the problems that you must discuss and solve together:

1. What kind of political rights are you willing to give the free blacks? The victorious northerners are insisting that you give freedmen the vote and let them participate in government. How far do you want these freedoms to go? Will you allow the blacks to be your equals in every way?

2. What kinds of rights will you give blacks in society? Can they own property? Travel freely? Get an education? Have any jobs they want?

3. How will you rebuild the economy of the South? How will you make up for the loss of free labor now that you don't own slaves?

4. How do you convince the North that you won't cause any more trouble for them? What will you do about the people in the South who are saying, "Save your confederate money; the South will rise again!"? How do you rejoin the Union and give up all that you fought for? What will you do with the Northerners who want to come to the South and "help you rebuild"? Some of them want to buy up your land and businesses and run for office in your state.

Group C: Freedmen

You can hardly believe it! You rejoice because the long, hard days of slavery are over. It seems like you have died and gone to Heaven. You are still on Earth however, and now you must face the unknown life of freedom after slavery. How will you survive on your own with no one to help you? How can you make a better life for yourself? Here are the problems you must discuss and solve together:

1. Who will you be? Do you keep your master's old name or make a new one? Do you try and find your lost family members separated by war and slavery or strike out on your own?

2. What kind of work will you do? Most of you know only farming. If you want to remain farmers, where will you get land? Will you try to get an education or some job training to improve your living conditions? Will you stay where you are and try to find work with your former master or go to the North or West to find new opportunities?

3. How much do you want to get involved in politics? They tell you that you can vote now, but how? Who will teach you to read? Who will explain the political system to you? You aren't familiar with political power because you have never had it before. Do you dare to run for office and try to change society yourself?

4. You face a lot of resentment and discrimination from the former leaders of the South. How will you get along with them peacefully? How can you solve your differences with them when some say that they will never treat you as an equal and want to restore things to the way they were before the Civil War? How will you protect yourself if things get violent?

Group D: Moderate Republicans

You have saved the Union at all costs. That included defeating the Confederacy and freeing the slaves. How hard will you be with the defeated South? You feel strongly that if you push them too far they will only rebel again. What kind of society will you set up now? Do you try to let all groups have complete social and political freedom or is freedom from slavery enough? Some groups resent your use of the president's power to make these sweeping changes. They miss the times before the war when Congress made most of the decisions. Others think that you are not acting quickly or strongly enough to deal with the problems at the end of the war. They want to punish the South and give complete freedom to blacks immediately. How will you keep a balance that will keep everyone happy and keep your party in power? Here are the problems you must discuss and solve:

1. How can you let the rebellious southern states rejoin the Union and be sure that they will stay loyal to the United States? How will you deal with the defeated Confederate Army leaders? Many are calling for their deaths as traitors. What will you do with your prisoners of war? How long will you keep troops in the defeated southern states? Your supporters want them removed as soon as possible to get things back to normal as quickly as you can.

2. How will you deal with the collapsed economy of the south? Will you rebuild it with northern money or let them fend for themselves? What do you do with the numerous unemployed former slaves? How will you treat the free blacks that want to move to the North and the West?

3. Do you have the right to tell the southern states how treat the free blacks? Will you change their laws and constitutions if necessary? Some of your fellow northerners have offered to go to the south and buy their farms and businesses and run their political offices if the southerners can't be trusted. Will you allow or encourage this?

4. How do you help protect the freed blacks from discrimination and racial violence? How do you educate blacks and find them jobs? How can you provide land for blacks who want to continue farming? How do you force Southerners to treat blacks as equals?

Taking Colonies Teacher's Guide

Objective: This activity is done individually as a creative writing assignment, but it still carries the spirit of this book in the sense that the student must assume the role of another and write from their point of view.

Duration: 1 class period.

Materials: Hand out a copy of the Taking Colonies handout to everyone.

Procedure: Discuss with students what the backgrounds of some of the people listed below might be. Let them choose which person they will write about.

Teacher Recommendations:
1. Remind them to stay within the proper time period and avoid anachronisms.

2. Also point out that a person might have had mixed feelings about taking colonies. They might have liked it for some reasons and not liked it for others. They also might not have felt like taking colonies mattered to them one way or another.

3. Tell your students that most of all they should be honest and write as that person would have felt not as a modern person would feel.

Taking Colonies: A U.S. History writing assignment

Description: The year is 1895. The U.S. does not yet have colonies or overseas possessions. You hear a politician give a speech saying that it is time that America join other great countries and take overseas lands to rule as their own. He says that this would bring the U.S. wealth through new trade opportunities, new jobs, and a source for goods not found in the U.S. He says that colonies would make us seem more powerful to other countries and give us the chance to civilize and Christianize the natives of distant lands.

Choose one of the people from the list below. Imagine that you are one of these people. How would they feel about taking colonies? How would it affect them? Would they have any special reason why they would think that colonies would benefit America or them personally, or would they be against it? Perhaps they have mixed feelings or feel that it wouldn't make any difference to them personally. Use your imagination and write as they would think.

- A housewife from Chicago
- A maid from Milwaukee
- A farmer from Kansas
- A naval captain from Maine
- A sailor from Seattle
- A rabbi from Boston
- A banker from L.A.
- A fisherman from Portland, Oregon
- A Protestant minister from Philadelphia
- A shipbuilder from Newport, Rhode Island
- A Mexican farm worker from San Antonio
- The U.S. ambassador to England
- A recent Chinese immigrant from San Francisco
- A sewing machine manufacturer from New York

Great Powers Game Teacher's Guide

Objective: To understand the issues and challenges leading up to the First World War.

Duration: 2-3 class periods.

Materials: A copy of the rules for each student. At least one copy of the country description sheet for each group. A large number of tokens in four colors representing the pieces for armies, navies, industries, and colonies.

Procedure:
1. Sides may be chosen in whatever way the teacher chooses, but it is usually better to give them out at random because not all countries start out even, just as it was in the real race for empire.

2. Go over the rules with the students.

3. Students read their country's description sheet and plan their strategy for diplomacy, economic, military, and territorial expansion.

4. Conduct negotiations.

5. Conduct wars and further negotiations as necessary.

6. Debrief.

Teacher Recommendations:
1. Encourage students to do the best they can even if they have a weak country. Weak countries can still win the game if the have the right allies. If the class is very large make up additional statistic sheets for small countries which remained officially neutral in W.W.I such as Mexico, Portugal, or Spain.

2. This game can be played without pieces, but the pieces make the record keeping easier. Appoint students to sell and collect the pieces. Watch for cheating! It is very important to tell the alliances NOT to combine their stacks of pieces because all too often alliances fall apart and it is too hard to go back and figure out who had what at the beginning.

3. If a war is declared simply list the country on the board that started it and the country that is being attacked. Then ask who would like to declare for each side. Allow a few minutes to allow reluctant stragglers to commit or stay neutral and for some countries to change

sides at the last minute if they wish. (This often happens in real wars). Once the numbers are tallied eliminate forces on both sides until there is clear victor. Armies cancel out other armies, and navies cancel out navies. The countries that started the war should always take the heaviest losses.

4. If all of the armies are gone, go to navies as a tiebreaker. Two navies equal one army when they land and convert to marines. If there is still no victor, go on to another round of negotiating and purchasing until another year of war is fought. Countries may change sides any time they want or drop out. You may even have multiple alliances going at each other at the same time. The only thing that matters is who is left the strongest when the fighting is over.

5. After the war is over the victors hold a peace conference and dictate the terms to the losers. These are up to the victors to decide, but they may include occupying or annexing the loser's home country, taking their colonies or a portion of their industry. If the losers stay unoccupied they may try to rebuild, make new alliances and seek revenge. Sometimes the victors may disagree on the fair share of the spoils and turn on each other in the next round of war. Continue the simulation until there is a clear victor or a hopeless stalemate and then move on to the debriefing.

Debriefing:

1. How did it feel to build your empire? How did the smaller countries feel about how it turned out? Which countries had the advantage at the beginning of the game? Why? How did your empire compare to the real one that your country actually gained?

2. In the long run what was more important to buy, armies, navies, industry or colonies? Why?

3. What did you do well? What do you wish you had done differently?

4. How successful were your alliances? Did they help you or hurt you? Could they be trusted? Why or why not?

5. If there were wars how did they compare to the real W.W.I? How would the world be different today if the war had turned out differently than it did?

Great Powers Game

Time: circa 1900

Players: Great powers of Europe, rising powers of Europe, America, and Asia, and lesser powers who wish they were great.

Goal: Make your country powerful by building industry, gaining colonies, building a strong army and navy and gaining strong allies. That way if a war breaks out you can win it.

How long the game is played: Each turn will represent one year. We will play until we reach 1920 or the Great War breaks out, whichever comes first.

How the game is played: Each player will represent one country. You will try to make your country as powerful as possible based on what you have to work with and your ability. Each country has a description sheet stating its strengths and weaknesses at the start. You will try to use the countries' income and your bargaining ability to gain further power and influence. Some countries are naturally bigger and richer at the start. This cannot be helped, so do the best that you can with what you have. Sometimes small countries do very well by growing and making the right friends.
You will continue to gain power, wealth, and influence until a war breaks out and then you must defend it. Try to make as many friends as possible so that you have allies if a war breaks out. Make written treaties whenever possible because people tend to "forget" what they promised. You can give, take, trade, or promise whatever you want and you don't have to tell anyone except the country you sign the treaty with. Remember how you treat people because "what goes around comes around", in other words if you always make threats or bully people around you may find yourself with very few friends when conflict breaks out. Remember, no matter how big you are, you can't take on everybody!

Spending your money: You may choose each year how to spend your money. Try to keep a balance. For example: don't spend so much on colonies that you have no army to defend them, or don't spend so much on the navy that you don't have any industry. Any money that you spend on industry or colonies stays in your economy each year, any money that you spend on the military is gone forever. In other words, if you buy a dollar's worth of industry or 1 colony your income goes up 1 dollar the next year. If you spend 1 dollar on the army or navy your income stays the same next year. So obviously, if you spend all your money on the military your country can never grow and everyone else will eventually pass you up.

Colonies: Whereas you can buy an unlimited amount of industry or military, there are a limited number of colonies to go around so try to get them early if you can. There are exactly 120 colonies available, not including the ones that you have at the start of the game. When the colonies are all gone you will have to fight with someone to take theirs away. Also be aware that certain countries have an interest in certain parts of the world and that taking a colony there will make that country upset with you. How you settle your disputes with other countries over colonies is up to you.

Wars: When 3 or more great powers are at war the war is considered a Great War. This war is fought by all countries that have existing treaties with the countries. War is done simply by counting up the forces of the groups of allies and declaring a winner. Note: a country can break a treaty and change sides or drop out of the war just before it takes place if they want to regardless of what they promised before. The forces in the war are recounted and then the war is fought. This is not a great way to gain friends and influence in the future however.

GREAT BRITAIN

Location: NW Europe
Size: small
Power: great
Friends: England has been an ally of just about every country in Europe at one time or another, but she prefers democracies to monarchies.
Enemies: England has been an enemy of just about every country in Europe at one time or another, but her most recent war was with Russia. It has been a long time since England has fought Spain, France or the U. S.. and she is hoping that those old hatreds are forgotten by now. There have been some disputes with France and Germany in recent years over colonies, but things seem to be getting better.
Goals: England's primary goal is to keep a balance of power in Europe. She does not want to let any one power dominate the continent. She has pledged to defend neutral countries like Belgium if any larger country tries to take them over. England will also try to defend free and unrestricted trade at all costs.
Strengths: England has the most powerful navy in the world, and everyone knows it. She also was one of the first countries to industrialize so she has a strong economy. England also has the biggest colonial empire in the world.
Weaknesses: England's many colonies require a huge army to keep them under her control. This leaves a very small army to defend England or to be used to attack other countries.
Income: 4 economic points per year.

Beginning Setup

Army: 1
Navy: 3
Industry: 3
Colonies: 3

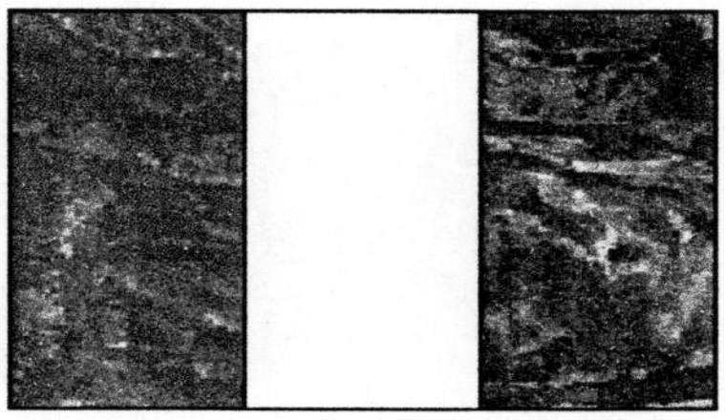

France

Location: W. Europe
Size: large
Power: great
Friends: France has no real allies, but has fought on the side of just about every country in Europe at one time or another when facing a common enemy. France prefers democracies to monarchies.
Enemies: All Europe remembers when Napoleon's armies tried to conquer the whole continent in the name of exporting France's democratic revolution and overthrowing kings and emperors. This has left most countries resentful of France because they did not like someone else telling them what kind of government to have. There have been some disputes with England in recent years over colonies, but things seem to be getting better. Germany and France fought a bitter war in 1870 in which Germany stole 2 of France's provinces. France has sworn revenge and says that some day Alsace and Lorraine will be taken back by force if necessary.
Goals: Defend France at all costs. Stop German expansion and reclaim lost lands. Expand colonial empire to rival that of England.
Strengths: Powerful army that is feared and respected. Good navy. She also was one of the first countries to industrialize so she has a strong economy. France also has the second biggest colonial empire in the world.
Weaknesses: France's many colonies require a large army to keep them under her control. This leaves fewer forces to defend France or to be used to attack other countries.
Income: 3 economic points per year.
Beginning Setup
Army: 2
Navy: 2
Industry: 2
Colonies: 2

Germany

Location: Central Europe
Size: large
Power: great
Friends: Germany has no real allies, but has a certain friendship with Austria because of the rulers being of Germanic ancestry. Germany's Kaiser is related to the King of England and the Czar of Russia. Germany prefers monarchies to democracies. Germany has a lot in common with Italy because both countries unified later than most of their neighbors; leading to fewer colonies and later industrial development.
Enemies: Most countries resent Germany's claims of superiority and threats to its neighbors. France, Denmark and Austria have lost territory to her in recent years. There have been some disputes with England and France in recent years over colonies, but things seem to be getting better. Germany and France fought a bitter war in 1870 in which Germany stole 2 of France's provinces. France has sworn revenge and says that some day Alsace and Lorraine will be taken back by force if necessary. Russia is afraid of German expansion because the Germans have expressed an interest in taking Poland away from her because part of it was once German.
Goals: Attack weaker neighbors whenever possible. Prove to the world that Germany is great through quick, decisive use of new military power. Hold on to recent German territorial expansion and add new lands to it if possible. Expand colonial empire to rival that of England and France.
Strengths: Powerful army that is feared and respected. Strong navy which rivals England for the first time ever. Rapid industrialization with a growing economy.
Weaknesses: Few colonies. Few allies. Army and navy are anxious to try their strength so they are not very patient or willing to compromise.
Income: 3 economic points per year.

Beginning Setup

Army: 3
Navy: 3
Industry: 2
Colonies: 1

Italy

Location: Southern Europe
Size: medium
Power: great
Friends: Italy has no real allies, but has fought on the side of just about every country in Europe at one time or another when facing a common enemy or when it thought that joining the right side would help it gain power and influence. Italy generally prefers democracies to monarchies. Germany has a lot in common with Italy because both countries unified later than most of their neighbors; leading to fewer colonies and later industrial development.
Enemies: Most countries resent Italy's refusal to commit to long-term alliances as Italy has changed sides many times in the past. Italy hates Austria for controlling large parts of northern Italy before Italy's unification. Austria has lost territory to Italy in recent years, and the Italians still feel that some of the territory under Austria's control should rightfully be theirs. The same is true for Italy's relationship with France, but they do not hate the French as intensely. There have been some disputes with England and France in recent years over colonies, but things seem to be getting better.
Goals: Italy is jealous of its more powerful neighbors and wants to be like them. Italy will stay out of wars if possible to avoid being on the losing side and losing territory. Italy will join a war if they feel that other countries will reward them for their help. Italy wants to hold on to recent territorial expansion and add new lands to it if possible. Expand colonial empire to rival that of England and France.
Strengths: Average army and navy that are yet to be proven. Gradual industrialization with a growing economy.
Weaknesses: Few colonies. No permanent allies.
Income: 2 economic points per year.
Beginning Setup:
Army: 2
Navy: 2
Industry: 1
Colonies: 1

Austro-Hungarian Empire

Location: Central Europe, Balkans
Size: large
Power: great
Friends: Austria has no real allies, but has a certain friendship with Germany because of the rulers being of Germanic ancestry. Austria prefers monarchies to democracies. Austria has a lot in common with Russia because both countries have conservative monarchies which have joined to fight off the territorial expansion of Germany and France.
Enemies: Austria has lost territory in recent years to Italy and Germany as a result of their unification movements. As a result it has focused its attention on taking over small countries in the neighboring Balkan Peninsula. Austria faces a major challenge because Russia would like to expand into this area as well to gain access to warm-water seaports. The two countries have nearly fought each other in a major war many times by backing up the small country the other was trying to take over. Another enemy is the Ottoman Empire because many of the small countries Austria is trying to take over once belonged to the Turks and the Turks want them back.
Goals: Attack weaker neighbors whenever possible. Prove to the world that Austria is still great by gaining control of the Balkan Peninsula by standing up to Russia, Germany, Italy and the Ottoman Empire. Hold on to recent territorial expansion and add new lands to it if possible.
Strengths: Average army that is still strongest in immediate area.
Weaknesses: The army is tied down by trying to keep many ethnic minorities within the empire from breaking away through revolution or foreign intervention on their behalf. Few colonies. Few allies. Many rivals. Small navy and a weak economy.
Income: 2 economic points per year.

Beginning Setup:

Army: 2
Navy: 1
Industry: 1
Colonies: 1

Russia

Location: Eastern Europe
Size: large Power: great
Friends: Russia has no real allies, but has a certain friendship with Germany and England because Germany's Kaiser is related to the King of England and the Czar of Russia. Russia prefers monarchies to democracies. Russia has a lot in common with Austria because both countries have conservative monarchies which have joined to fight off the territorial expansion of Germany and France.
Enemies: Russia is afraid of German expansion because the Germans have expressed an interest in taking Poland away from her because part of it was once German. Russia faces a major challenge from Austria because both countries are interested in taking over the Balkan Peninsula. The two countries have nearly fought each other in a major war many times by backing up the small country the other was trying to take over. Another enemy is the Ottoman Empire because many of the small countries Russia is trying to take over once belonged to the Turks and the Turks want them back. Russia also faces competition in Eastern Asia from Japan because both countries are interested in taking over parts of China. England has vowed to contain Russian expansion in Asia. As if this were not enough, revolutionaries at home are threatening to overthrow the Czar and form a democratic or communist government.
Goals: Russia would like to expand into the neighboring Balkan peninsula and take over small countries as well to gain access to warm-water seaports. Hold onto vast empire and avoid war whenever possible. Prove to the world that Russia is still great by gaining control of the Balkan Peninsula by standing up to Austria, Germany, England, Japan and the Ottoman Empire. Hold on to recent territorial expansion and add new lands to it if possible.
Strengths: Huge army that is still feared and respected. Vast colonial empire.
Weaknesses: Army weakened by old-fashioned equipment and techniques and need to put down rebellions by colonies and revolutionaries. Small navy. Few allies. Many rivals. Small navy and weak economy.
Income: 3 economic points per year. Beginning Setup
Army: 3
Navy: 1
Industry: 1
Colonies: 2

Ottoman Empire

Location: Balkans, Western Asia
Size: large
Power: great
Friends: Turkey has no real allies, but has a certain friendship with France because they often have the same enemies. They also admire Germany's military power and share some of their enemies. Turkey prefers monarchies to democracies.
Enemies: Turkey has lost territory in recent years to Italy, France, England, Russia, and Austria which it would like to reclaim. Turkey faces a major challenge because Russia would like to expand into its territory to gain access to warm-water seaports. The two countries have fought each other in small wars many times. Another enemy is Austria because many of the small countries Austria is trying to take over once belonged to the Turks who want them back.
Goals: Hold onto vast empire and avoid war whenever possible. Prove to the world that Turkey is still great by regaining control of the Balkan Peninsula and lost North African colonies. Standing up to the challenge from the other great powers to conquer the remaining Ottoman Empire and divide it amongst them. Hold on to what is left of your empire and add new lands to it if possible.
Strengths: Average army. Many colonies.
Weaknesses: Army is tied down in trying to keep more colonies from breaking away from you than already have. Few allies. Many rivals. Small navy and weak economy.
Income: 2 economic points per year.

Beginning Setup

Army: 2
Navy: 1
Industry: 1
Colonies: 2

United States of America

Location: North America
Size: large
Power: great
Friends: U.S.A. has no real allies, but has a certain friendship with France and England because of democratic traditions and because they often have the same enemies. The U. S. strongly prefers democracies to monarchies.
Enemies: U.S.A. has no real enemies, but will fight against an enemy it feels is morally wrong. The U.S.A. has had some minor disputes with England, France, and Germany over colonies in South America and the South Pacific, but has avoided war every time.
Goals: Although America usually stays out of other countries' affairs, it is beginning to be interested in keeping a balance of power in Europe and Asia. She does not want to let any one power dominate either continent. America is eager to demonstrate new power and influence. America will also try to defend free and unrestricted trade. The U. S. is mostly interested in neutrality, but America will pick a fight with someone who tries to keep them from trading with either side in a war.
Strengths: Strong army and navy. Plentiful resources and rapid industrialization have given it a strong economy.
Weaknesses: Few allies. Reluctance to get involved in foreign affairs, especially wars.
Income: 4 economic points per year.

Beginning Setup

Army: 2
Navy: 2
Industry: 3
Colonies: 1

Japan

Location: East Asia
Size: small
Power: small
Friends: Japan has no real allies, but has a certain friendship with England because they often have the same enemies. Japan usually prefers monarchies to democracies however.
Enemies: Japan is in direct competition with Russia for domination of the Chinese Province of Manchuria. They have almost gone to war over it several times. Japan has had some minor disputes with England, France, and Germany over colonies in China, but has avoided war every time.
Goals: Although Japan usually stays out of other countries' affairs, it is beginning to be interested in keeping a balance of power and establishing colonies in Asia. She does not want to let any one Western power dominate Asia. Japan would like to have Asia to itself, but is not yet strong enough to try and take it from the Western Powers. Japan is eager to demonstrate its new power and influence. Japan is mostly interested in neutrality, but will pick a fight with someone who tries to keep them from gaining colonies.
Strengths: Small army and navy. Rapid industrialization is giving it a growing economy.
Weaknesses: Few allies. Reluctance to get involved in foreign affairs, especially European wars.
Income: 2 economic points per year.
Beginning Setup
Army: 1
Navy: 1
Industry: 1
Colonies: 1

Army

Army

Army

Army

Army

Army

Army

Army

Army

Army

Army

Army

Army

Army

Army

 Navy	 Navy	 Navy
 Navy	 Navy	 Navy
 Navy	 Navy	 Navy
 Navy	 Navy	 Navy
 Navy	 Navy	 Navy

Industry

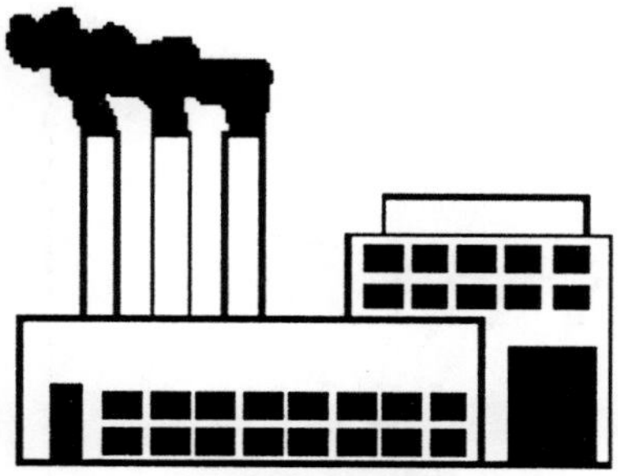

Industry

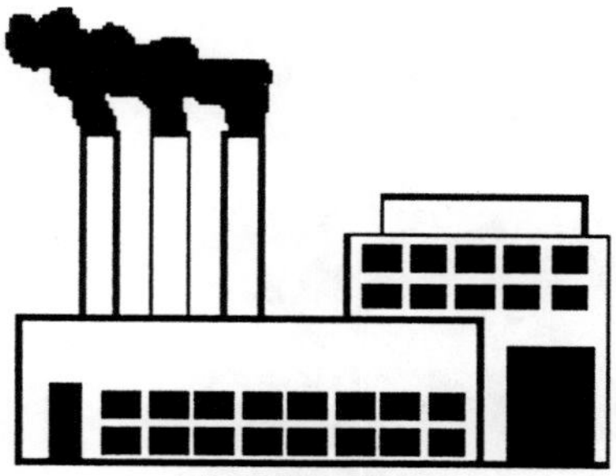

Industry

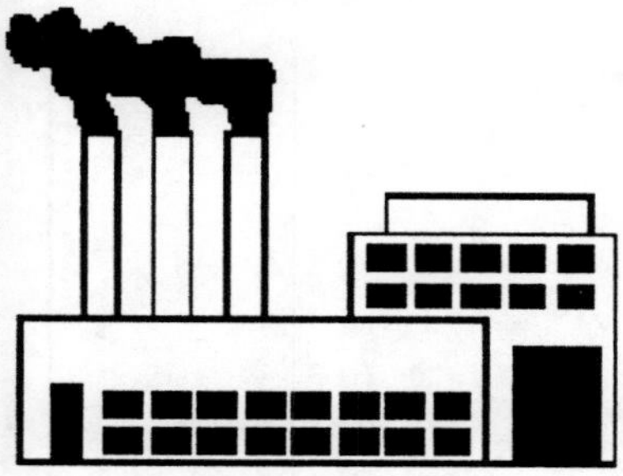

Industry

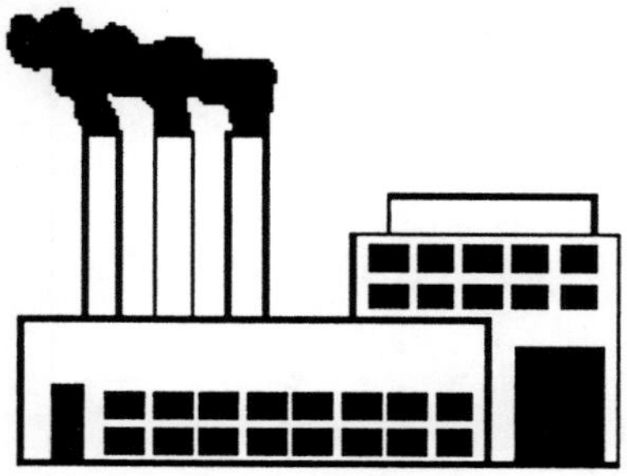

Industry

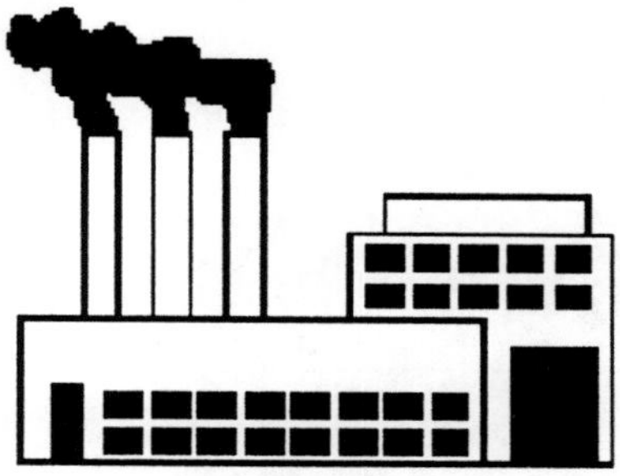

Industry

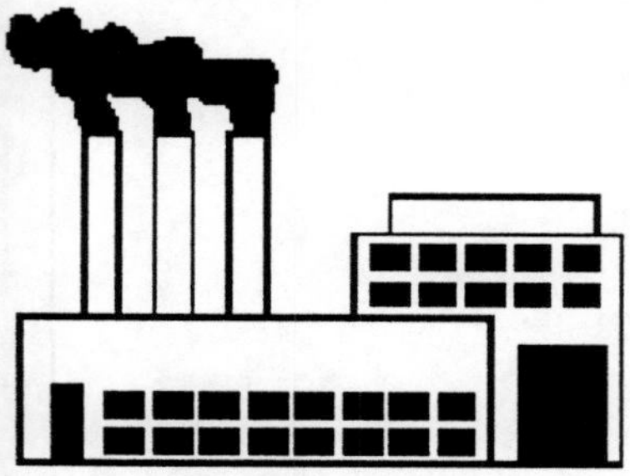

Industry

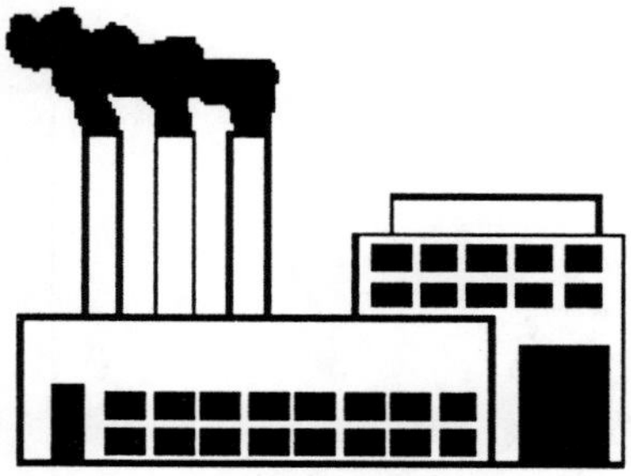

Industry

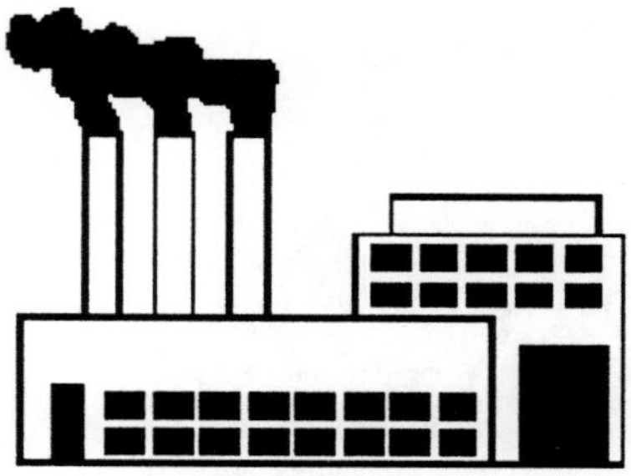

Industry

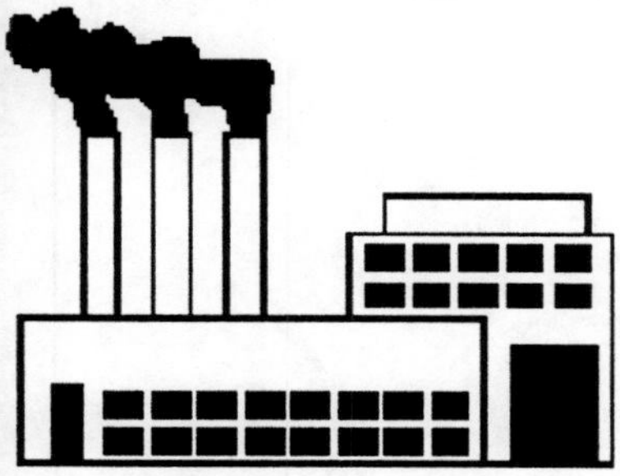

Industry

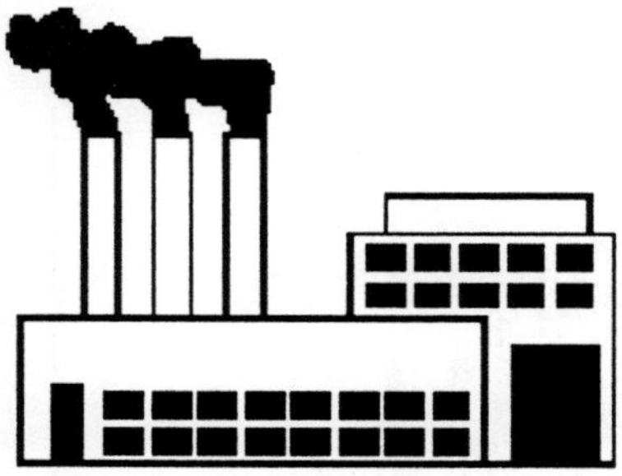

Industry

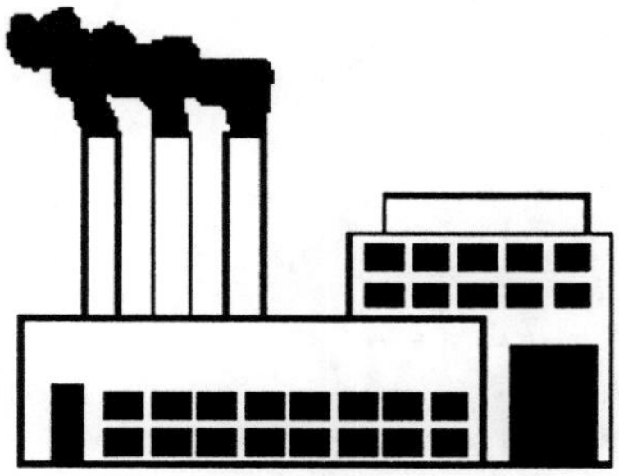

Industry

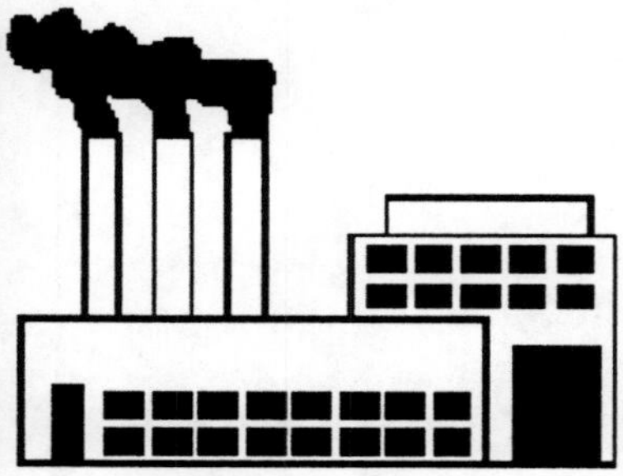

Industry

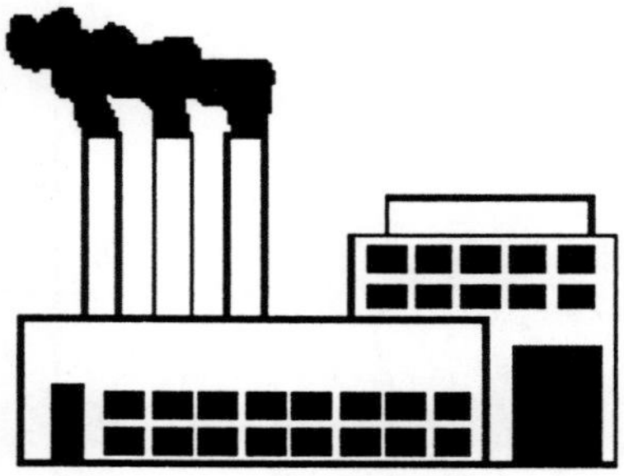

Industry

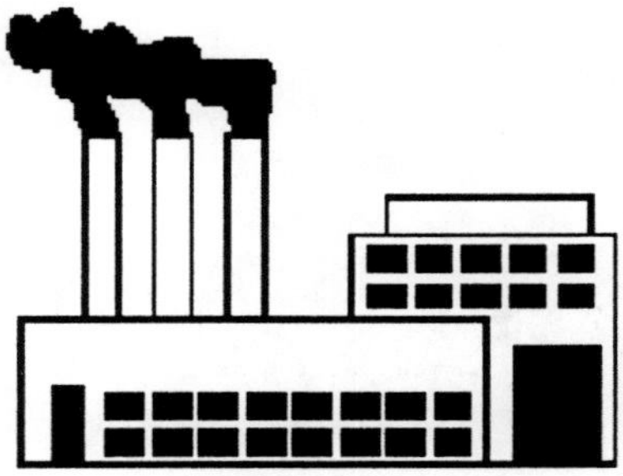

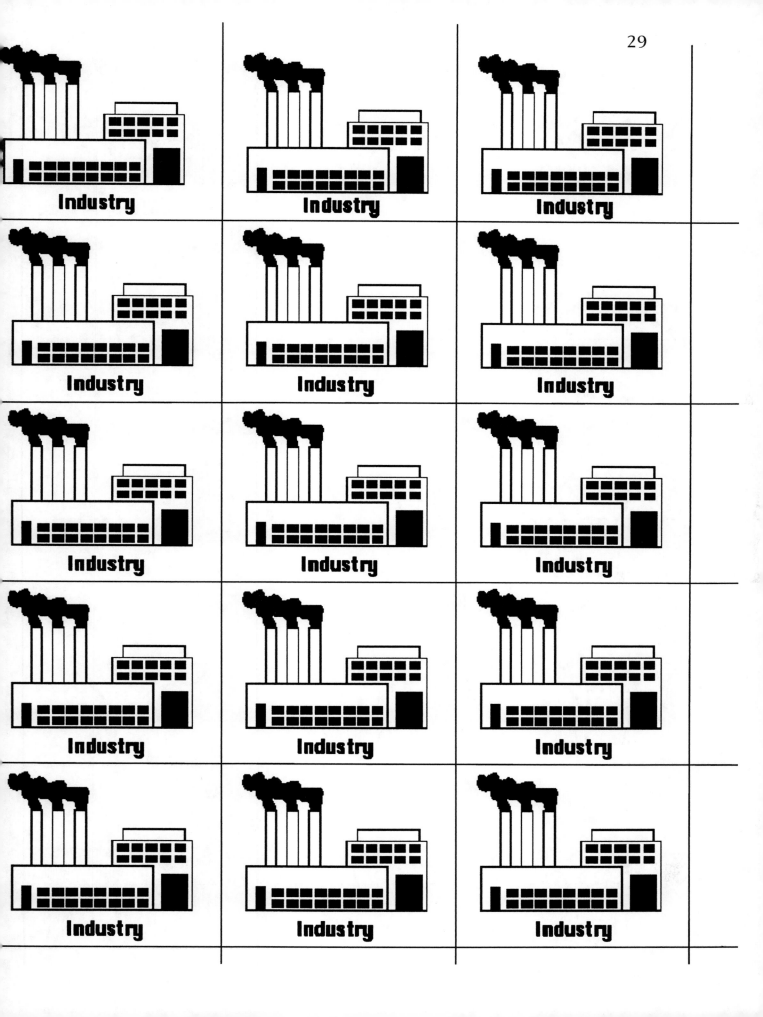

Industry

Congo

Taureg

Kambara

Tchad

Sokoto

Abyssinia

Madagascar

Morocco

Maurctania

Orange Free State

Nigeria

Tunis

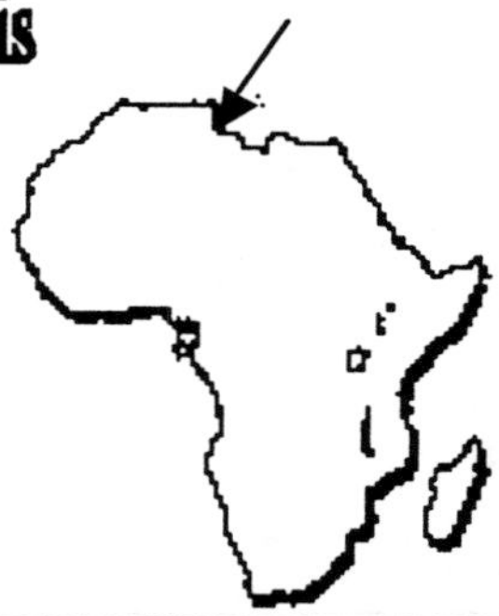

Algiers

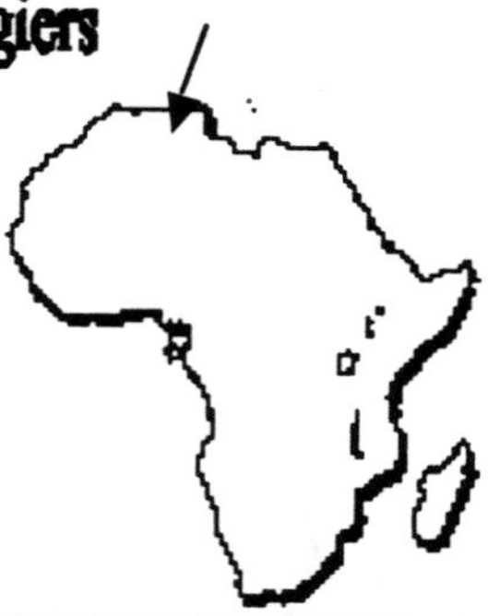

Mozambique

Angola

Ashantee

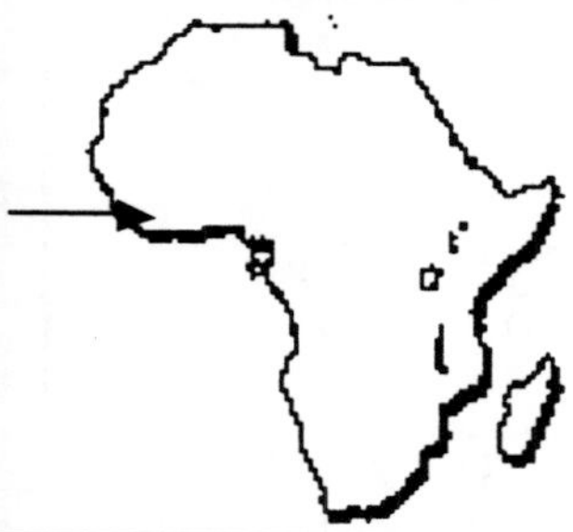

Bechuanaland

Rio de Oro

Cape Colony

Berbera

Rhodesia

Egypt

Senegambia

Kambara

Eritrea

Gold Coast

Gabon

Algiers

Somalia

Sudan

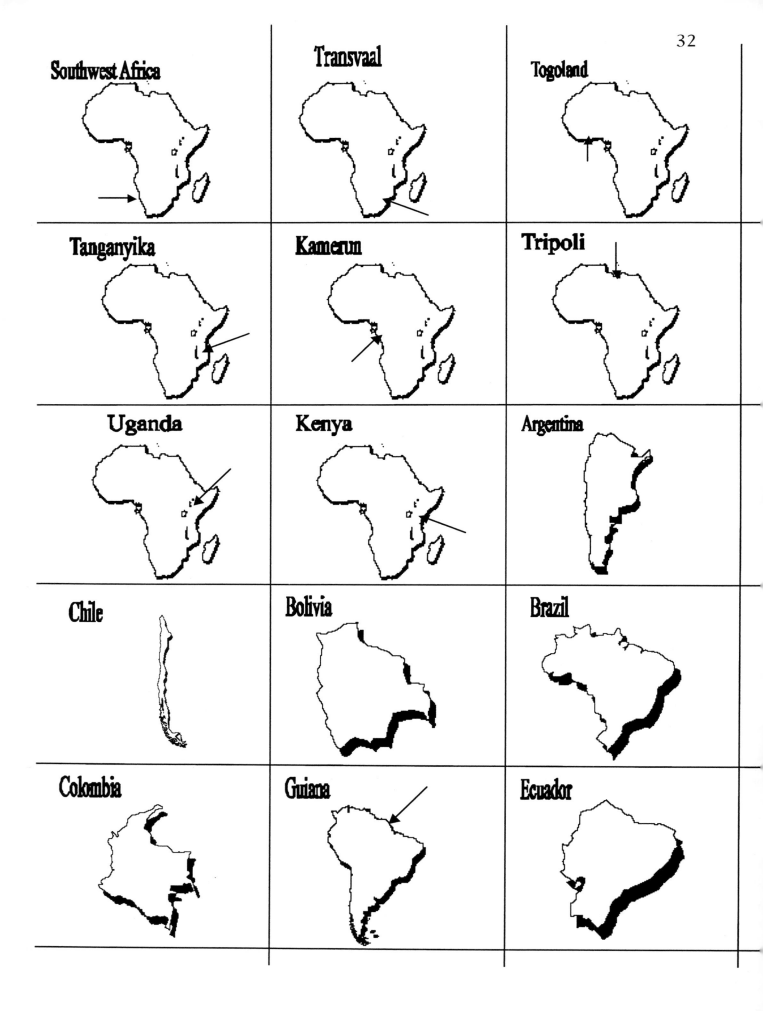

Southwest Africa

Transvaal

Togoland

Tanganyika

Kamerun

Tripoli

Uganda

Kenya

Argentina

Chile

Bolivia

Brazil

Colombia

Guiana

Ecuador

Australia

New Zealand

New Hebrides

New Guinea

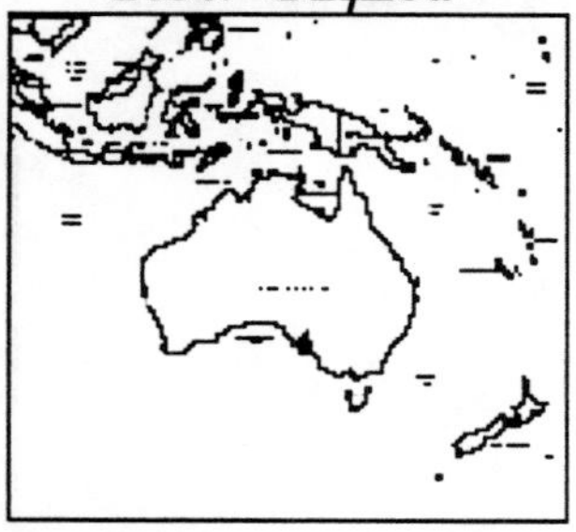

Bismarck Archipelago

Papua

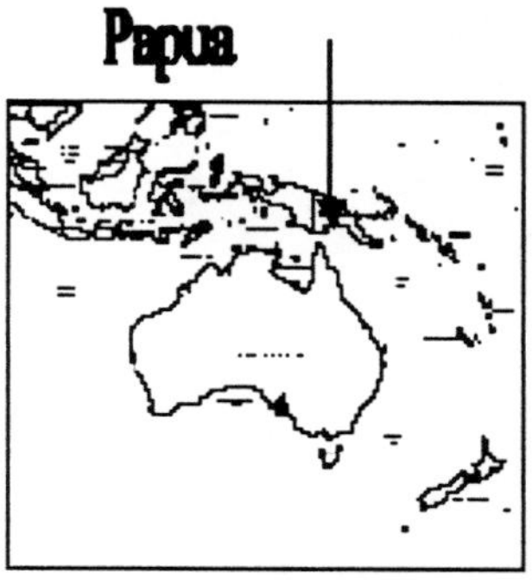

Dutch East Indies

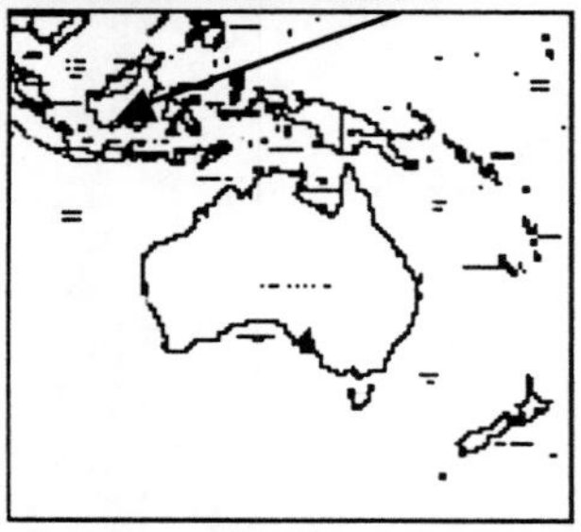

Fiji

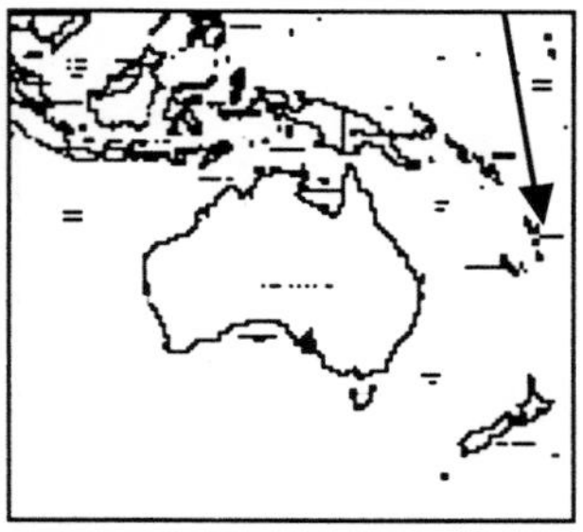

Samoa

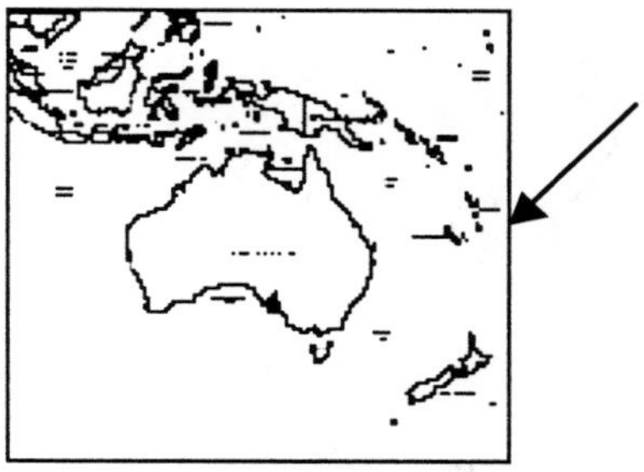

New Caledonia

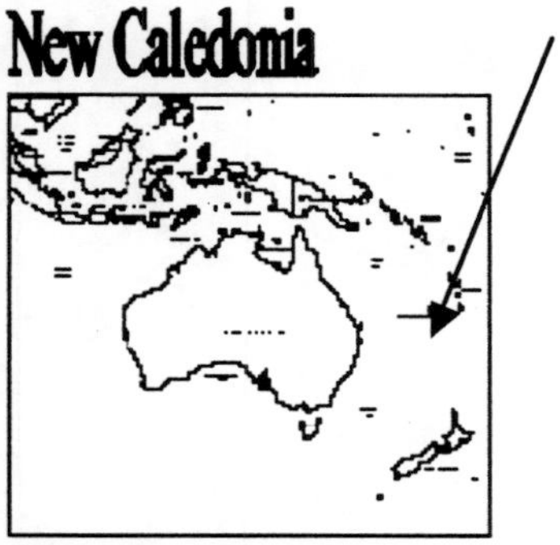

Kaiser Wilhelm's Land

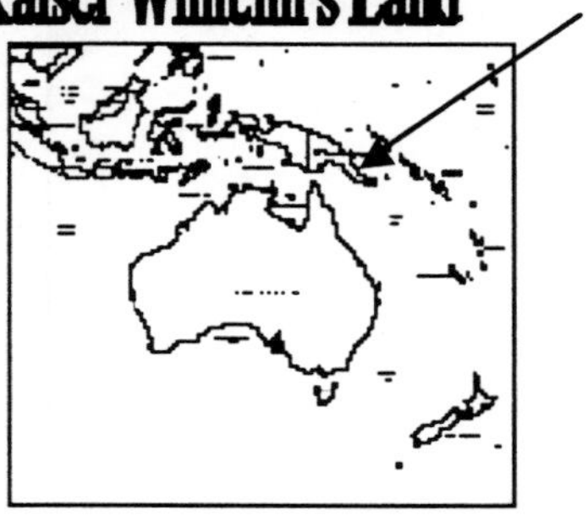

Sarawak

Solomon Islands

Philippines

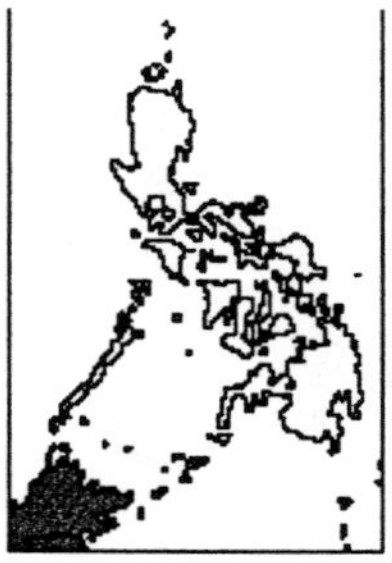

Hawaii

Siam

Burma

Formosa

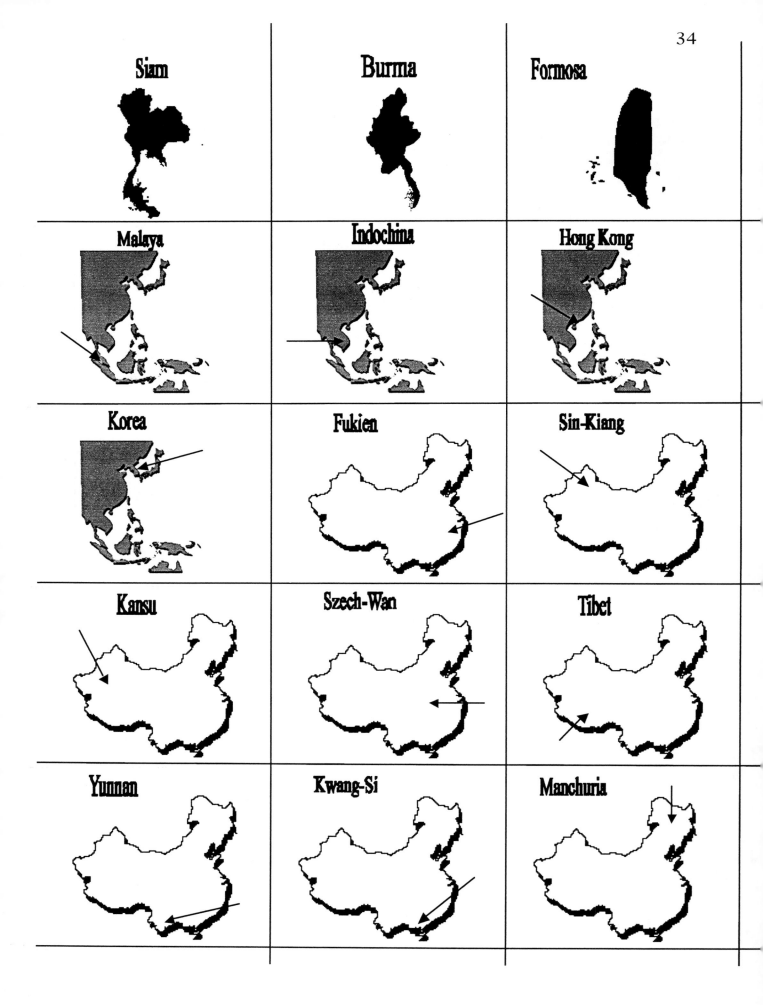

Malaya

Indochina

Hong Kong

Korea

Fukien

Sin-Kiang

Kansu

Szech-Wan

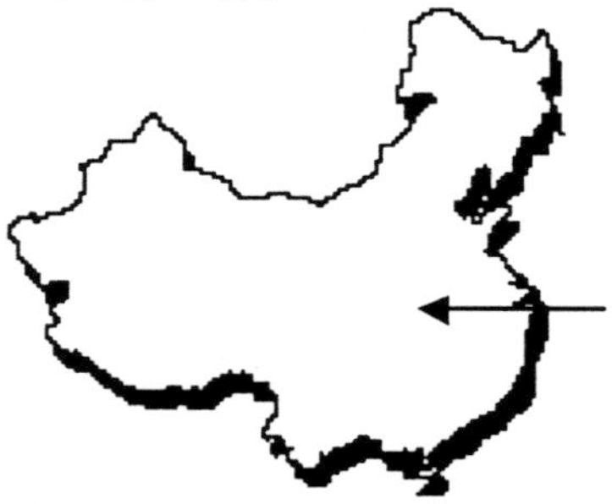

Tibet

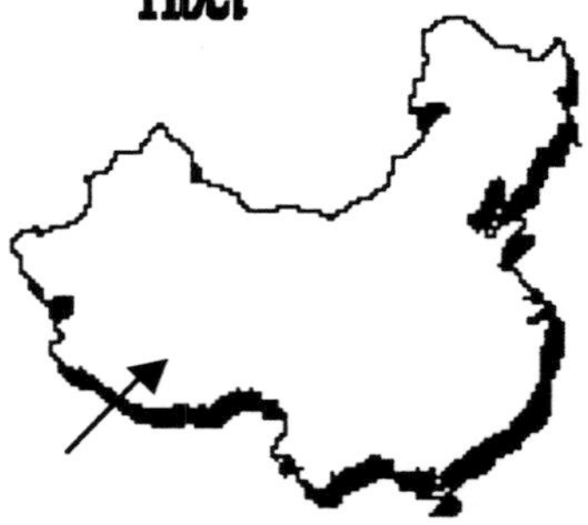

Yunnan

Kwang-Si

Manchuria

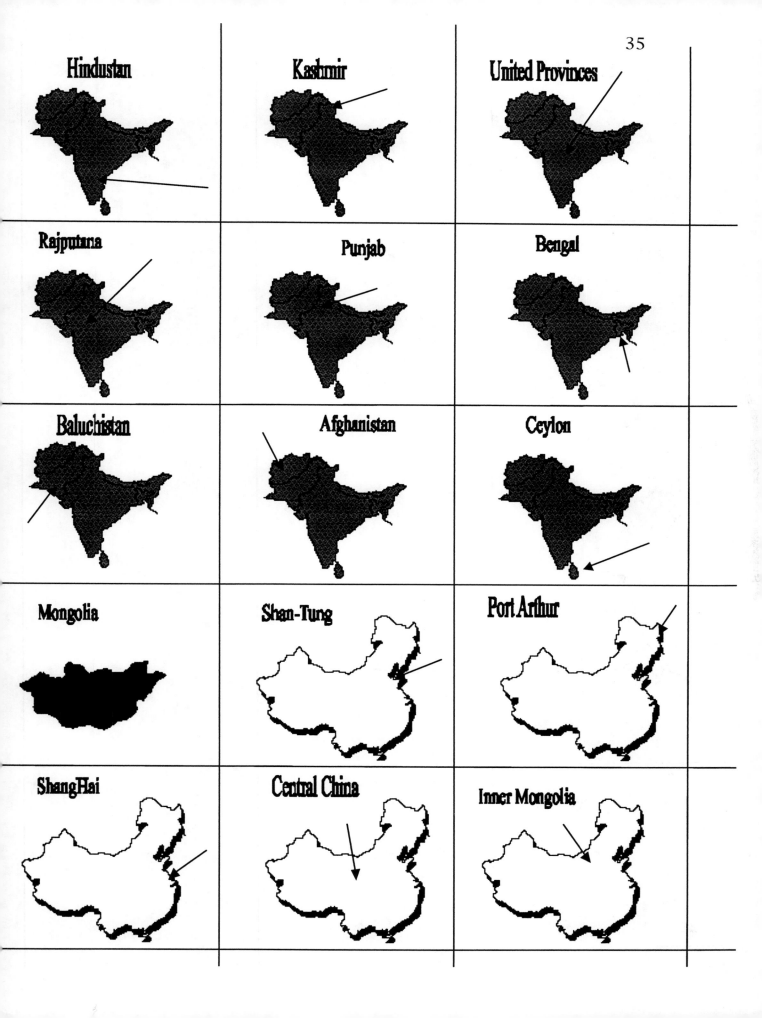

Hindustan

Kashmir

United Provinces

Rajputana

Punjab

Bengal

Baluchistan

Afghanistan

Ceylon

Mongolia

Shan-Tung

Port Arthur

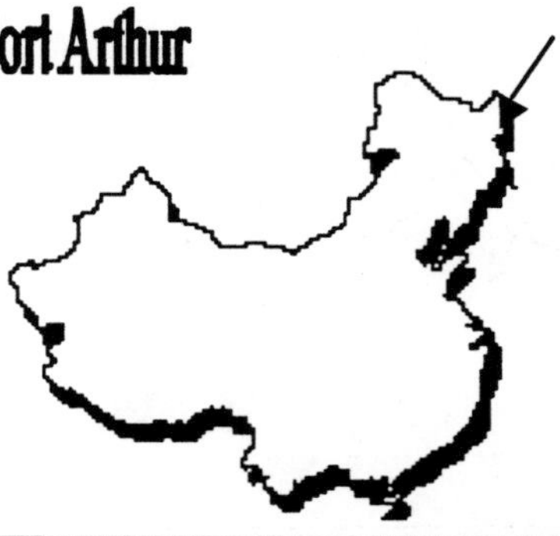

ShangHai

Central China

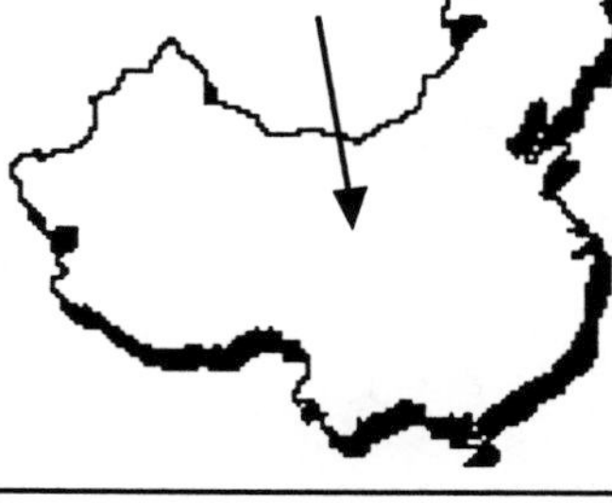

Inner Mongolia

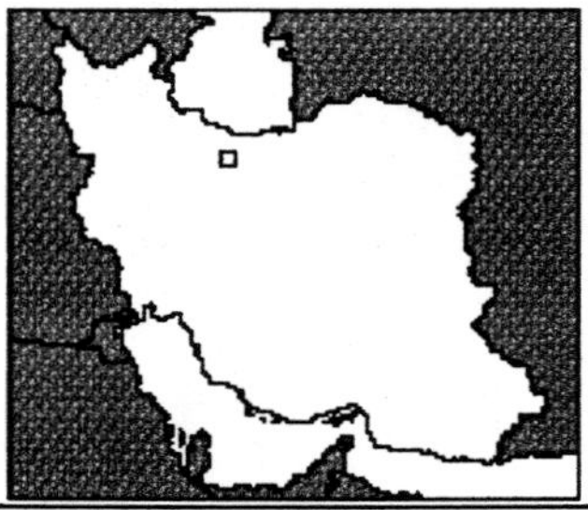
Persia

Turcomania

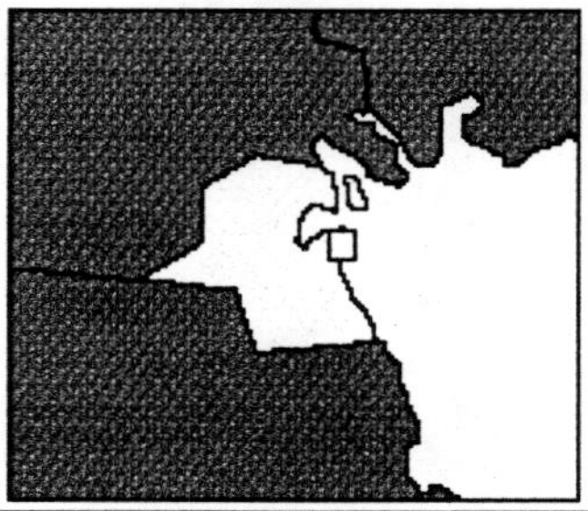
Kuwait

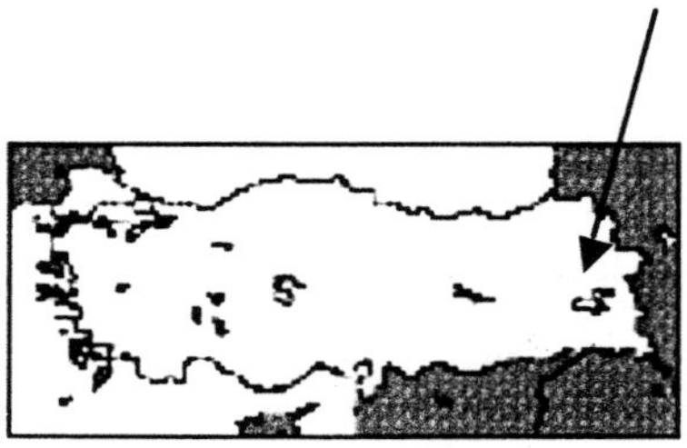
Anatolia

Aden

Greece

Serbia

Bulgaria

Rumania

Cuba

Puerto Rico

Haiti

Dominican Republic

Bahamas

Virgin Islands

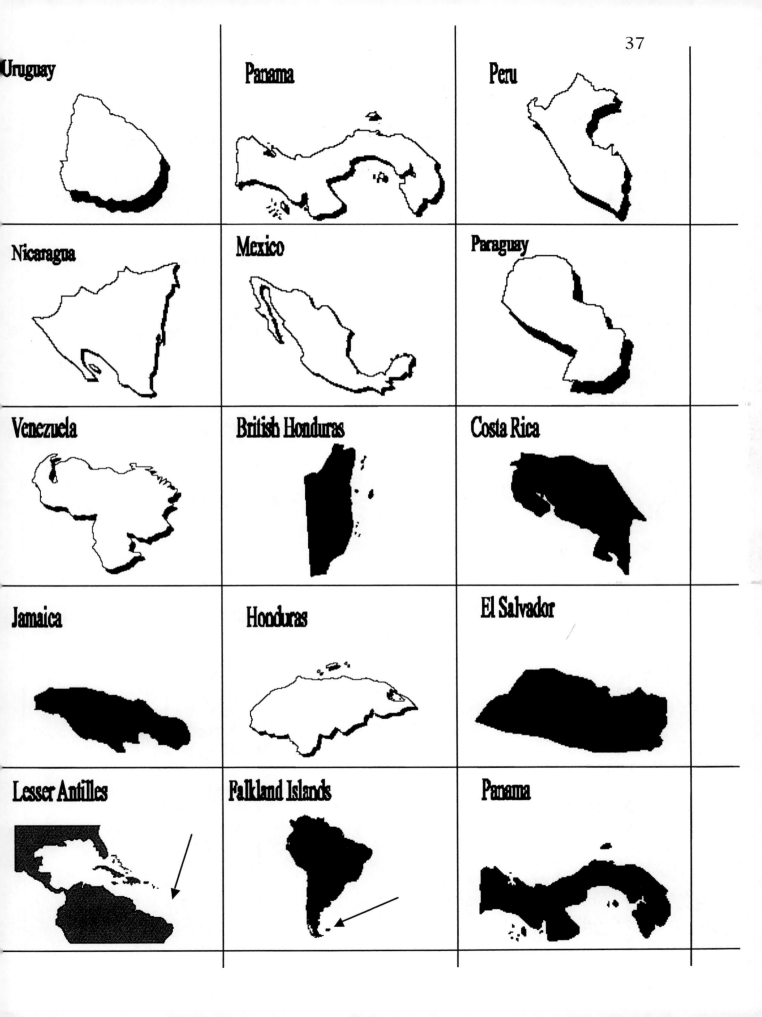

Uruguay

Panama

Peru

Nicaragua

Mexico

Paraguay

Venezuela

British Honduras

Costa Rica

Jamaica

Honduras

El Salvador

Lesser Antilles

Falkland Islands

Panama

STRIKE! Teacher's Guide

Objective: Students will learn a lot about how collective bargaining and the strike tactics of labor and management work.

Duration: 2-5 class periods.

Materials: Materials: Run off enough copies of the simulation description for everyone, and enough of each groups role for each group. Calculators and plenty of scratch paper are also helpful.

Procedure:

1. Divide the students into groups representing labor, management, and if desired, special interests.

2. Conduct planning sessions, bargaining, and contract negotiations.

3. Role-play the contract approval or consequences of a strike.

4. Complete calculations to see if both sides are still profitable.

5. Repeat the above steps as necessary until there is a clear winner, a signed contract, or a hopeless stalemate.

6. Debrief.

Teacher Recommendations:

1. This is a lively simulation that involves planning, bargaining and good old fashioned number crunching.

2. Be careful not to tell the students too much in advance about how to resolve their conflicts. They will learn far more by working it out for themselves. After the simulation is over bring up any tactics that may have been left untried such as hiring scabs, blacklisting, walkouts, sit-downs, sick-ins, sabotage, hiring thugs or security forces, lockouts, company unions, closed and open shops.

3. This simulation may be played by two or three groups depending upon the size and ability level of the class. The last page, which covers special characters, may be added as an additional challenge for a talented group or as away to incorporate additional students.

4. You as the teacher need to play the role of all outside authorities such as government officials etc.

5. It is very important to stress the need for good record keeping for this activity. Lazy groups that don't do their record keeping are usually taken advantage of by the sharp-eyed accountants of the other group. Have students turn in their records and any contracts signed as a part of the grade for the assignment.

6. While it is true that anything could and did happen when a strike occurred, try to keep a lid on the violent actions which students may suggest as a way out of their deadlock. These can make the simulation interesting, but are sometimes a bit difficult to role-play. You don't want to stifle their creativity, but remind them that violent actions have serious repercussions. (See the Golden Rule and similar sayings). While violence was often a part of real strikes, remind them that their primary goal is to negotiate a contract and that anything that distracts from that is bound to only make things worse.

7. Use your judgment as to how far you let students go with their role-playing depending upon their maturity and your comfort level. A truly open-ended simulation is the most fun, but are you really prepared to handle playing the police, courts, etc.? (Keep in mind that the authorities usually sided with the company in a dispute whether they had been bribed to do so or not due to class similarities and the pro-business nature of the law in those days). What about how this will effect the relationships of students in your class? The payoff can be great, but are you willing to take the associated risks?

Debriefing:

1. What were the tactics used by each side in the simulation? How are these similar to those described in your textbook or those that the teacher has told you about?

2. How successful was your group? What worked well? What might you have done differently? What benefits were earned for the workers? Are there any that you could have asked for given more time? (Health care, hourly pay, minimum wage, holidays, weekends, paid vacations, childcare, profit sharing, accident insurance, better working conditions, competition for the company store etc.)

3. How good was your leadership? What could they have done better? Could you do better?

4. How did this strike compare to the real strike in 1921? (See the book by Mildred Beik listed below. The only thing agreed to after over a year on strike was the right to unionize).

5. How did this simulation compare to other labor disputes in your own area or time?

6. How do you think that you might react if you were caught in the middle of a labor dispute in the future?

STRIKE!

A Simulation of Labor-employee Relations

Characters: The Berwind-White Coal Company Board of Directors,
The United Mine Workers Union Bosses

Object: To make the most money and set up the best conditions for your side.

How it works: The class will be divided up into teams, which will compete with each other for power, influence, and money. There are no benefits whatsoever for the workers at the beginning, so everything must be bargained for in whatever way works best for you. The Company on the other hand has no requirements on what they must pay the workers or how they must treat them. Their only requirement is to make as much money as possible while maintaining sensible business practices to avoid going out of business. Both sides will learn the art of compromise or find out that the consequences of conflict may be more than you bargained for.

Each side has basic financial needs they must meet and anything beyond that is up to them to gain any way they can. The winner is the team or teams that do the best job of managing their side successfully. The losers are those who don't get what they want or lose their jobs as leaders of their group. Smaller groups will represent other elements of society such as non-mining company employees, strikebreakers, and elements on either side of the law.

Where and when: This is a simulation of labor conditions in western Pennsylvanian coal mining towns of about 1921. All facts and figures provided are based on those taken from Senate Document #633 1909-1910, The Immigrant Commission: "The Immigrant in Industry", Beik, Mildred A., *The Miners of Windber: Class, Ethnicity, and the Labor Movement in a Pennsylvania Coal Town, 1890's-1930's,* and from local oral histories.

Employer's Needs

1. In order to produce 50,000 tons of coal it will take 3,000 miners 5 days of work at 8-hour days.
2. Workers must receive a minimum of $3.00 a day to meet their living expenses. If they are paid less than that they will leave town and find work elsewhere.
3. Workers are paid by the ton of coal produced not by the hour or day worked. The going rate is $1.28 a ton for coal. The company does not pay for so-called "dead work" which involves cutting away and hauling the rock to get at the coal or loading the coal and bringing it to the surface. Different miners work at different speeds and some days would get them no pay at all. All the company is interested in is in the coal, if it takes more than 8 hours a day to dig the average of 3.33 tons produced daily, then the miners must make up the hours on their own without additional pay.
4. At the start of the simulation the Company has a 50,000-ton surplus of coal in storage.
5. The Company must pay a basic operating cost of $10,000 a week to operate and maintain its machinery and to pay for shipping costs for the coal.
6. Any miners employed at the start of the simulation will already have paid for their own equipment. New miners hired will have to pay one dollar for new equipment and will work at only 50% of the productivity of regular workers for the first week of employment while they are in training.
7. Accidents do occur. On the average there is a 5% chance of an accident in the mines each week. If scab or replacement workers are being used in the mines the accident rate is doubled for one month. With each accident between 1-20 workers will be killed or injured from cave-ins, explosions, gas poisonings, or dangerous equipment. The occurrence of accidents can be determined by the roll of a percentile die. These workers must be replaced by the Company which means that they will need training etc. At the start of the simulation there is no compensation in pay for injured or dead workers as a result of accidents on the job.

You must decide:
1. what kind of wages and benefits you will give the workers
2. the length of the workday
3. the number of workdays in a week
4. how you will handle worker demands and how you will respond to possible strikes, violence etc.

It is necessary that you keep records of your team's weekly financial standing in order to see if you are making a profit or not. It is suggested that you use something like the following example:
Price of coal $10.41 a ton x 10,000 tons = $104,100
Price paid to miners $ 1.28 a ton x 10,000 tons = $12,800 daily wages
Weekly expenses $10,000 ÷ 5 days = $2,000 daily expenses

$104,000 income
-$12,800 wages
-$2,000 expenses

$89,000 daily profit

Make adjustments as necessary when the price of coal or workers' demands change your costs. Then give weekly totals to compare how you are doing over the course of time. This will help you determine how much of pay raises you can give the workers and what price you can charge for the coal.

Workers' Needs

1. You must make $3.00 a day to cover your basic living expenses and support your families this includes:

a. rent and furnishings (.50 ¢)

(The company owns the homes and pays the utilities)

b. food ($2.00)

c. mining equipment and clothing (.50 ¢)

Any additional miscellaneous personal expenses and special purchases must be bought on credit from the company store.

2. Workers are paid by the ton of coal produced not by the hour or day worked. The going rate is $1.28 a ton for coal. The company does not pay for so-called "dead work" which involves cutting away and hauling the rock to get at the coal or loading the coal and bringing it to the surface. Different miners work at different speeds and some days would get them no pay at all. All the company is interested in is in the coal, if it takes more than 8 hours a day to dig the average of 3.33 tons produced daily, then the miners must make up the hours on their own without additional pay.

3. Be careful how long you go on strike:

a. You can go 1 week without pay, but this will use up all of your personal savings.

b. If a strike extends into a second week the workers start to go into debt to the Company Store because it's the only place where you can shop in town. At the beginning of the third week the Company will begin to deduct your charges from your future pay once you do go back to work.

4. If you can't pay your debts after one month, you will have your line of credit cut and be forced to work for the company until your debts are paid off. In other words, you are stuck in this town until you pay up. If you don't pay your debts you can go to jail or skip town and become a fugitive from the law.

5. At the start of the simulation you have:

a. no benefits

b. no job security

c. no contract

In other words, everything must be negotiated. If you don't ask, they are not going to give it to you!

6. Accidents do occur. On the average there is a 5% chance of an accident in the mines each week. If scab or replacement workers are being used in the mines the accident rate is doubled. With each accident between 1-20 workers will be killed or injured from cave-ins, explosions, gas poisonings, or dangerous equipment. The occurrence of accidents can be determined by the roll of a percentile die. These dice are available at most hobby or game stores. These workers must be replaced by the Company which means that they will need training etc. At the start of the simulation there is no compensation in pay for injured or dead workers as a result of accidents on the job.

It is necessary that you keep records of your team's weekly financial standing in order to see if you are making a profit or not. It is suggested that you use something like the following example:

Price of coal paid to miners \$ 1.28 a ton x 10,000 tons = \$12,800 daily wages

\$12,800 daily wages x 5 days = \$64,000 weekly wages

\$3.00 a day living expenses x 3,000 miners x 7 days = \$63,000 weekly expenses

 \$64,000 wages
-\$63,000 expenses

\$1,000 weekly profit ÷ 3,000 miners = .33¢ a week profit per miner

Make adjustments as necessary when negotiations change your wages. Then give weekly totals to compare how you are doing over the course of time. This will help you determine how much of pay raises you can ask for and how much money workers can afford to pay towards benefits or a strike fund.

Special Characters:

Day workers: Commonly known as Company men. Unlike the regular miners, you are native-born Americans and not immigrants. Your jobs have higher prestige and pay. You do skilled jobs such as accounting, carpentry, blacksmithing, machining and counting and loading coal. You earn about $7.50 a day instead of being paid by the ton. Your work is far less dangerous than the miners' and the company treats you better because you are harder to replace. You represent 630 of the 3000 miners in Windber.

The Strikebreakers: You are the most recent set of immigrants. You will take any job at any pay whether there is a strike going on or not. You don't trust unions and cannot afford to pay union dues. You number 5,000 strong and the company would love to put you in the miners' place if they get too troublesome. Their only worry is how to get you trained fast enough. Try to deal with them to see if they will hire you to replace the miners.

Coal and Iron Police: Private rail police experienced at busting heads and breaking up strikes. They are a legally-armed force, which is given a lot of leeway to keep the peace, as long as they obey the law. They are very expensive, but very effective. They can guard, protect, enforce lockouts, and disperse mobs.

The Hoodlums: These unemployed desperadoes can be hired to do just about any crime you can think of. They may be of use to the miners or the company depending on who pays them better. They will naturally be concerned as to who takes the rap if they get caught.

The Interborough Rapid Transit Company of New York:
You are mostly interested in keeping the subways running on time. If anything disrupts that you are concerned. The going rate for coal is $10 a ton, but you will gladly buy more if the price goes down. You cannot afford to pay more than $20 a ton for coal to break even with your operating costs. You need about 100,000 tons a week, but have other suppliers if Berwind-White's prices get too high.

The Government: All judges, police, city, county, state, or federal officials are played by the teacher.

W.W. II Debates Teacher's Guide

Objective: To understand the various controversies surrounding W.W.II both at the time and today.

Duration: At least 1 class period for the research. From 1-15 class periods depending upon the number of topics debated.

Materials: Hand out a copy of the W.W. II Debates handout to everyone. A good research library with access to both primary and secondary sources is necessary. Use of the Internet may be helpful, but be very careful to explain that these sites may be very biased and not always accurate.

Procedure:

1. Divide the students into 2-4 member teams of mixed ability levels.

2. Divide the teams into those who will defend a particular side of the issue or the other.

3. Research the topics.

4. Conduct the debates in class with members of other teams judging those who are presenting.

Teacher Recommendations:

These debates require research and a great deal of preparation. What makes them a role-playing experience is that the debate team members must argue one side of the issue even if they disagree with it. Historical roles may be assigned to the students, which they must act out in character. In that case, they must speak as those people would have spoken and know only about things they could have known about in 1945.

If not, the teacher may decide to allow the students to use information from new research about these events as evidence. Either way, team members must defend their resolutions regardless of whether or not they are personally in agreement with it. The teacher and students together should decide what kind of debate format and rules will be used and how the project is to be judged or evaluated.

Debriefing:

1. What did you learn from this experience?
2. If W.W.II was so long ago, why are these issues still so controversial today?
3. Is there ever agreement on the truth of what really happened in history?
4. How did it feel to defend a position you might normally be against?
5. What other topics would you consider for debate?

W.W. II Debates

1. Was it really necessary for the United States to enter W.W.II? Could the United States have remained neutral? Were we dragged into the war or did we enter willingly?

2. Did President Roosevelt conspire to get the US to enter W.W.II even though many were opposed to it? What actions did he take to prevent or join the war?

3. Was the Japanese attack on Pearl Harbor truly a "surprise attack"? Did the United States have any advanced warning of the attack? What could we have done to avoid it?

4. Was it necessary to place Japanese-Americans in internment camps during W.W.II? Should damages be paid to survivors of those camps? What about the Italian and German-Americans? Why weren't they detained?

5. Could the US have done more to prevent the Holocaust from happening in Nazi Germany? Did we act quickly enough or in the appropriate ways?

6. Was it necessary to drop the atomic bombs on Hiroshima and Nagasaki? Could the war have been brought to end in any other way at that time?

7. Was it necessary to insist upon unconditional surrender from the Japanese at the end of W.W.II?

8. Was the use of carpet bombing against our enemies in W.W.II necessary and ethical?

9. Did the United States treat the Soviet Union as an equal partner in W.W.II? Did our handling of the demands of the Soviets at the end of W.W.II lead to the poor relations that would develop into the Cold War? Did Roosevelt and Truman deal with Stalin properly?

10. What happened to the body of Adolf Hitler? How did he really die? Are the bones in the possession of the Russians authentic? What of the conspiracy theories claiming he survived the Fall of Berlin and went into hiding?

11. Should Japan apologize for its actions in W.W.II? Should compensation be paid to the citizens of its former colonies? Who is responsible and who should pay?

12. Should the personal property and money confiscated by the Nazis from Jews be returned to the survivors of the Holocaust and their descendants today? What if the funds were hidden in secret Swiss bank accounts that no one has claimed in all these years?

13. Should land occupied at the end of W.W.II by the victorious Allies be returned to the nations that lost them? Should they remain American or be given independence instead? Should Allied forces be completely withdrawn from countries occupied after W.W.II?

14. Should Nazi war criminals continue to be prosecuted and tried? If convicted, what kind of punishments should they be given?

15. What should be done about the Neo-Nazi movements in Germany and America? What about those who deny that the Holocaust ever took place?

Cold War Simulation Teacher's Guide

Objective: This simulation gives students a feel for the multiple levels of competition between the Superpowers during the Cold War. It helps them to realize that the way that the Cold War ended in the real world was not a foregone conclusion by any means.

Duration: 1-3 class periods.

Materials: Hand out a copy of the Cold War Simulation rules handout to everyone. Use a large world map that all can see. The pull down type is the best for visual effect, but any Cold War era world map could be made into a transparency for the game. Mark Communist countries and allies with a red sticker and those that were pro-USA in blue. Make sure that they are the kind that are easily removable like those round price stickers that they sell for garage sales. Start by marking the Superpowers and their staunchest allies circa 1945 and then add new stickers as countries declare for one camp or the other. The awesome sight of the whole world quickly filling up with colored stickers will give them a good sense for the geopolitics of the struggle and let them see where their next move should be.
Reproducible game pieces are provided at the end of this section of the book. Feel free to make as many as you need. It is a good idea to have several dozen of each kind cut out and stored in separate envelopes before the game. It is also very helpful to designate a couple of students to help you hand out and collect pieces during the game.

Procedure:
1. Divide the students into three teams, The United States, The Soviet Union, and the nonaligned countries. (Approximately 5 minutes).

2. Teams plan their moves according to the rules of the simulation. (Approximately 5 minutes).

3. Teams negotiate with each other. (Approximately 5-10 minutes).

4. The teacher records students' moves on the map. (Approximately 5 minutes).

5. Resolve conflicts according to the rules of the simulation. Make any changes on the map that arise from wars. (Approximately 5 minutes).

6. Repeat the above steps until there is a winner or all of the teams have been eliminated. (See victory conditions in the rules that follow).

7. Debrief. (Approximately 5-10 minutes).

Teacher Recommendations:

1. Three groups are created by teacher's choice or at random. The neutral or nonaligned countries are the toughest to play because they may require a bit of prior knowledge to play in some cases. Some pre-reading on the subject or research by players on their countries could enhance the game. For the most part they just need to listen to both sides equally and support the side that promises them the most. Try and get them to think like the country they are playing. They do not want to be left out of the gift giving by the superpowers or left without allies if a war breaks out, but would like to stay neutral if at all possible. The best model is modern India, which has received aid from both, but never firmly committed to either the East or the West. For the purposes of this game neutral countries do not grow economically, they merely seek aid. They do not gain armies unless they conquer a neighbor or receive aid from a superpower. They usually do not activate their military forces unless attacked. They can not buy new armies or navies each turn and never develop nuclear forces on their own. If a neutral attacks another neutral of equal military strength the results are inconclusive unless they receive additional military aid from a superpower. The war continues to the next turn at which point either superpower may choose to intervene. For simplicity's sake some smaller nations have been combined into regions to increase playability, but it should be explained to students that in the real world even the tiniest neighbors might still be antagonists.

2. Caution students that the point of the game is to gain as much advantage over the other side as possible without being dragged into a war. If the Cold War turns into a "hot war" then everybody loses.

3. Coach the students on the various roles they can play within the group. This will help those less familiar with role-playing know what to do. Make sure everyone understands terms like hawk and dove before you begin.

4. The pace of the game will advance quickly once everyone grasps the concept. There are many ways to beat your opponent with war being only the last resort. Should a war actually break out then the Superpower that starts it must state whether it is a conventional war or nuclear. Simply list the country on the board that started it and the country that is being attacked (even if it was a neutral country that attacked another neutral country). Then ask who would like to declare for each side. Allow a few minutes to allow reluctant stragglers to commit or stay neutral and for some countries to change sides at the last minute if they wish. (This often happens in real wars). Once this is done, count up the number of armies, navies, and nuclear bombs and write them on the board in separate columns. The first force to be dealt with is the nuclear bombs the defender takes the first hits and then the attacker. (See rules for nuclear combat below). The country whose capitol is destroyed is immediately out for the rest of the game and any others subsequently attacked. Sometimes this will shock others into making peace and other times nations will fight on to the bitter end to seek revenge even if they know it means their own destruction. After any nuclear conflicts have been resolved the rest of the combat is resolved with conventional forces. Simply remove forces from each column as they cancel each other out. The side with the most forces remaining wins. If no side has a clear victory, the conflict goes on for another turn. If one side has only navies left and the other side has no forces left the navies may be converted into marines and invade in the same way as armies except at half strength.

Debriefing:

1. How real did this feel? Are you glad it turned out the way it did or terrified of the prospect? What would the world be like today if it had?

2. Why do you suppose the two superpowers felt they needed to compete in every area? What did they think would happen if they would lose?

3. Which of these areas of competition were tried in the actual Cold War and why? Which ones were most successful?

4. Who has the advantage at the beginning of the game? Who do you think usually wins? Who won the real Cold War? Why?

5. What would the world be like if the Cold War were still going on today?

Cold War Simulation

Purpose of the game: to understand the nature of competition between the Soviet Union and the U.S. during the Cold War.

Sequence of Play:
1. The US starts out with 75 points and the USSR 65. The teacher rolls one random event for each superpower on the random events chart and adjusts the map or point totals accordingly.
2. Each team chooses how their income will be spent. Deduct the number of income points spent from the total. A Superpower may purchase tokens that represent economic, food or military aid, to be given away to neutral countries. These tokens will later be distributed to neutral countries to gain their support. The Superpowers may also choose to spend their points on internal improvements that are listed below. Superpowers must spend all of their points each turn, but undistributed tokens may be spent on themselves.
3. After discussing among your team your choices for distribution, submit them in writing to the teacher. All moves are turned in simultaneously and take effect immediately. Once they are written down they cannot be changed. Each turn represents one year.
4. As countries declare their alliances place control markers of the appropriate color on the map and adjust the point totals and income for each superpower for the following year.

Rules:
There are three teams, The United States, The Soviet Union, and the nonaligned countries. The US and the USSR try to sway the neutral countries to their alliance to achieve world domination. This can be done through giving them economic, food or military aid, or by military conquest. The Superpowers may designate the number of tokens of each kind that they wish to give to a neutral nation. Those points are no longer part of that nations total. When a country agrees to become an ally of a superpower their strength points get added to the superpowers total. This number is also printed on that nation or region's card. Each country has a given number of economic, food or military aid points it desires before committing to one side or the other. This is printed on that nation or region's card. These numbers are merely goals however, the nation may agree to commit to one side or the other at any time they wish.

Domestic spending options for the Superpowers:

1. **Internal Development.** Each point invested in economic power increases the nation's income by one point the following turn and every turn thereafter. This is done by purchasing economic aid cards and spending them on your own country.

2. **The Arms Race.** These conventional military forces are the same as military aid cards but are retained by the superpower for use at home and abroad. They come in two types: armies or navies. A superpower must have at least one navy to deploy forces on another continent. One navy is needed for each new continent that may not be reached from your home country by land. Military power may be used in a conventional war against any country. If their defensive strength is overwhelmed the country becomes a satellite. If the other superpower tries to take the same country in the same year, a civil war breaks out, and the forces fight until there is a victor. Each turn new forces may be added. At any time a superpower may decide to withdraw or escalate the conflict to a nuclear one. Use of nuclear force removes a neutral country or region from the game permanently and may provoke a nuclear war with the other superpower if it has vowed to protect it.

3. **Nuclear arms.** Each nuclear arm purchased can be used to destroy the capital city of one country. A destroyed country is then out of the game. The other superpower may choose to retaliate with everything that they have by launching a nuclear attack of any kind, anywhere. If a superpower is the victim of an attack, they may only respond with 90% of their forces because some of their forces would be destroyed in the initial attack.

4. **The Space Race.** A country must invest in the space race if it wishes to build Intercontinental Ballistic Missiles. Each point spent on the space race increases your economy by one point.
1 card = long range bombers. Your country may now drop atomic bombs by air. This means that its planes may still be shot down by the enemy's conventional forces, however.
2 cards = rockets. You may use them to destroy the army of a neighboring country or deliver an atomic bomb to destroy their capitol
3 cards = medium range missiles. You may use them to destroy the army of any country on the same continent as you are or deliver an atomic bomb to destroy their capitol.
4 cards = long range missiles. You may use them to destroy the army of any country in the world or deliver an atomic bomb to destroy their capitol.

5 cards = moon landing. You are the envy of the whole world! Gain one free economic aid card, one free military aid card and add +1 to your economy.
6 cards = missile defense system. You may destroy one incoming enemy missile for each additional space card purchased from now on.

Victory Conditions:
The first superpower to reach 150 points or eliminate the other superpower wins the game. The neutral countries can win if both superpowers have been wiped out and they are still intact. It is possible for everyone to win if a nuclear war has been avoided and no countries have been destroyed. It is also possible for everyone to lose if a nuclear war has occurred and all countries have been destroyed.

Roles on a team:

Individuals on each team will play one of the following roles:

A. War hawk: pro-military, eager for a confrontation, looking for a showdown.

B. Doves: believe in peace at all costs, do not like war under any circumstances, especially fearful of nuclear war.

C. Diplomats: will always try to negotiate a compromise with the other superpower or try to persuade neutral countries to join your side.

D. Scientists: will try to advance knowledge of space.

E. Isolationists: are in favor of staying out of other countries' business.

F. Businessmen: want to have peace to trade with other countries, but like to sell things to the military too. Support whatever helps your nation's income.

G. Farmers: want countries where they can sell their food. They will sell food to just about any country they can.

H. Reformers: want to improve things at home first. Feel that wars are a waste of money.

I. Dissidents: people who are unhappy with their own government. They like the other superpower better and can be persuaded to defect to the other side, but it is usually more fun to stay home and complain all the time.

J. Patriots: people who love their country and feel that it can do no wrong. They have a hard time understanding why everybody doesn't want to be like them.

Random Events Table: **Roll a 20-sided die**

1- new invention	+1 economic point
2- technology becomes outdated	-1 economic point
3- bumper crop	gain 1 food aid token
4- crop failure	lose 1 food aid token
5- epidemic	-1 economic point
6- medical breakthrough	+1 economic point
7- revolution in neutral country of teacher's choice	reroll: 1-10 it becomes an ally of the US, 11-20 an ally of the USSR
8- revolt in neutral country or region of teacher's choice	lose 1 ally
9- labor unrest	-1 economic point
10- increase in productivity	+1 economic point
11- civil unrest	lose one military aid token
12- patriotic movement	gain one free military aid token
13- strong leader	+1 economic point and gain one free economic aid token
14- weak leader	-1 economic point and lose one free economic aid token
15- shortages/inflation	-1 economic point
16- surpluses/deflation	-1 economic point
17- scandal	lose one economic aid token
18-reform movement	gain one economic aid token
19- crime/drug problem	-1 economic point
20- law and order movement	+1 economic point

Economic aid

Economic aid

Economic aid

Economic aid

Economic aid

Economic aid

Economic aid

Economic aid

Economic aid

Economic aid

Economic aid

Economic aid

Economic aid

Economic aid

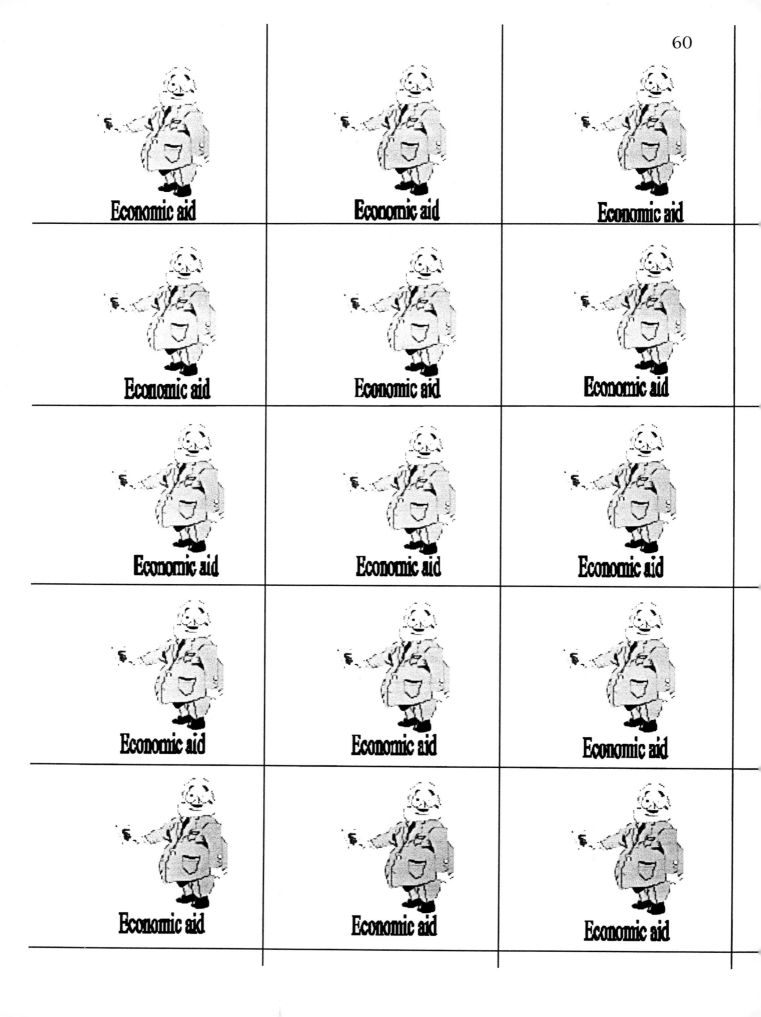

Economic aid

Food aid

Food aid

Food aid

Food aid

Food aid

Food aid

Food aid

Food aid

Food aid

Food aid

Food aid

Food aid

Food aid

Food aid

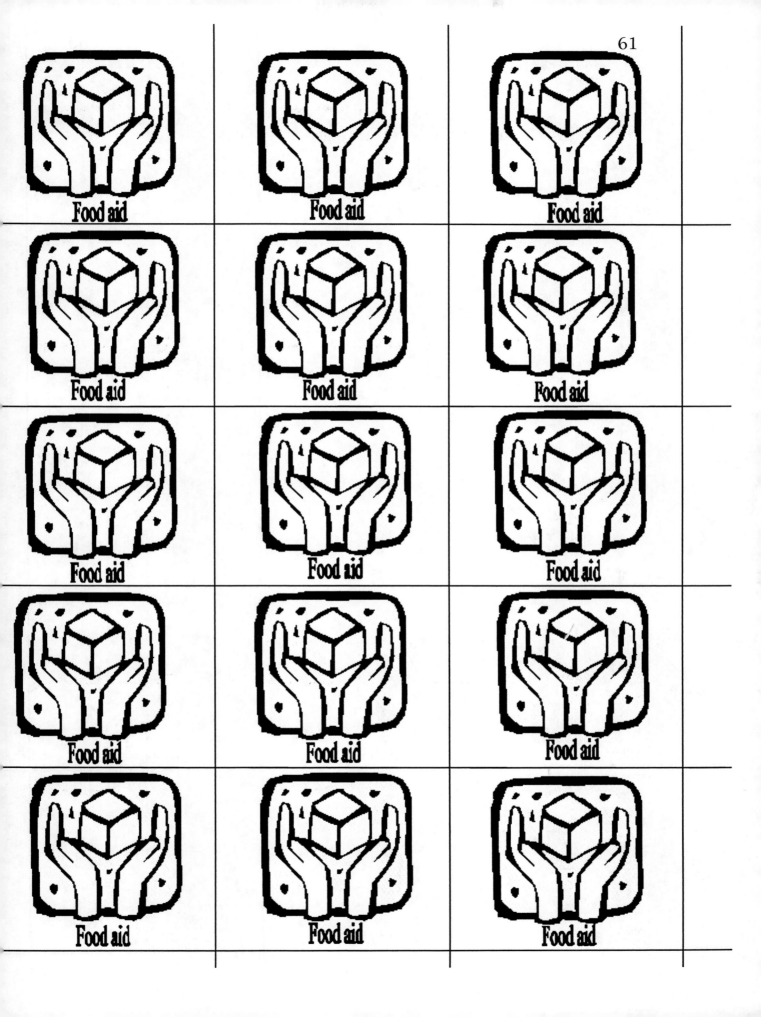

Food aid

Military aid

Military aid

Military aid

Military aid

Military aid

Military aid

Military aid

Military aid

Military aid

Military aid

Military aid

Military aid

Military aid

Military aid

Military aid

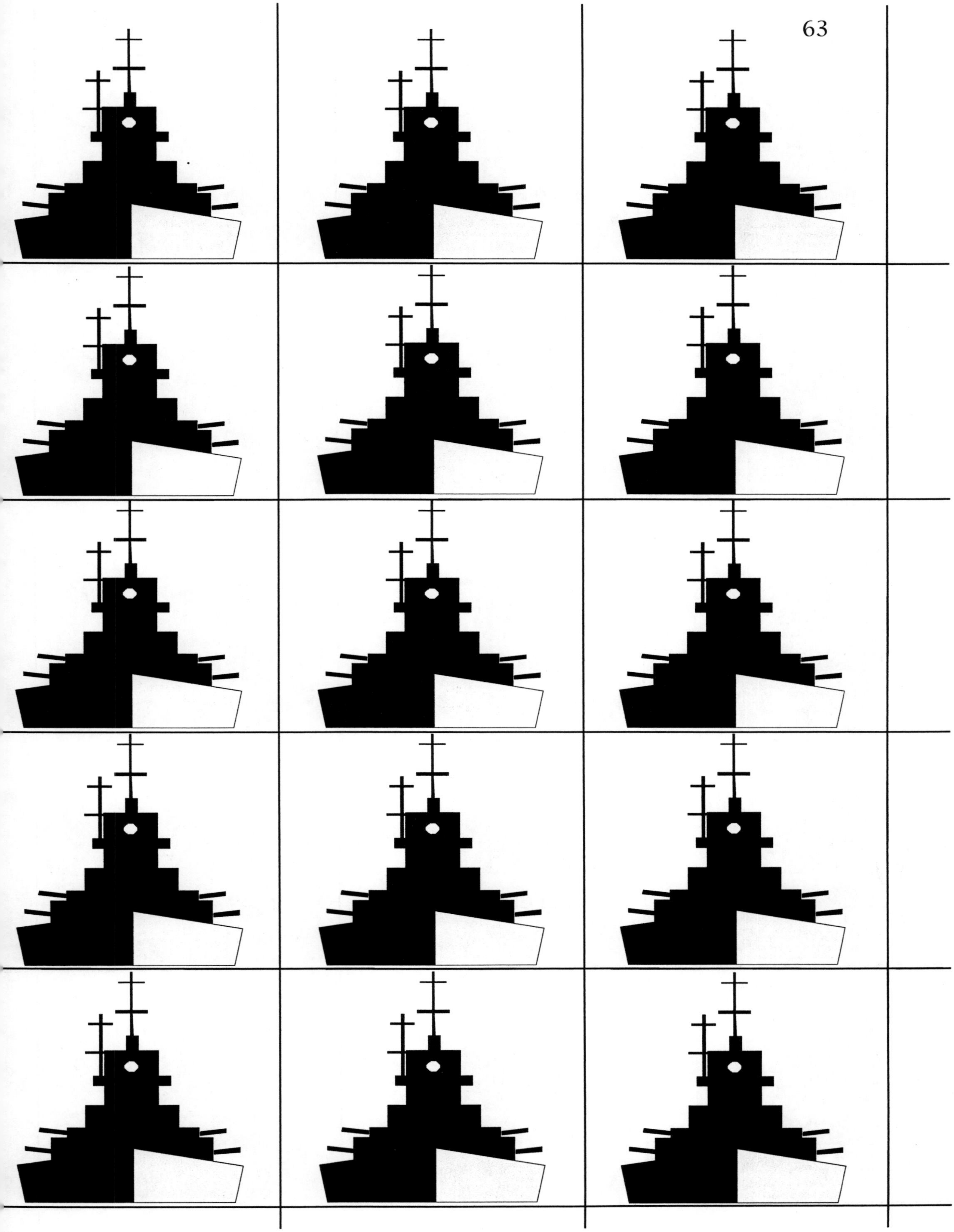

Nuclear bomb

Nuclear bomb

Nuclear bomb

Nuclear bomb

Nuclear bomb

Nuclear bomb

Nuclear bomb

Nuclear bomb

Nuclear bomb

Nuclear bomb

Nuclear bomb

Nuclear bomb

Nuclear bomb

Nuclear bomb

Nuclear bomb

Space Race

Space Race

Space Race

Space Race

Space Race

Space Race

Space Race

Space Race

Space Race

Space Race

Space Race

Space Race

Space Race

Space Race

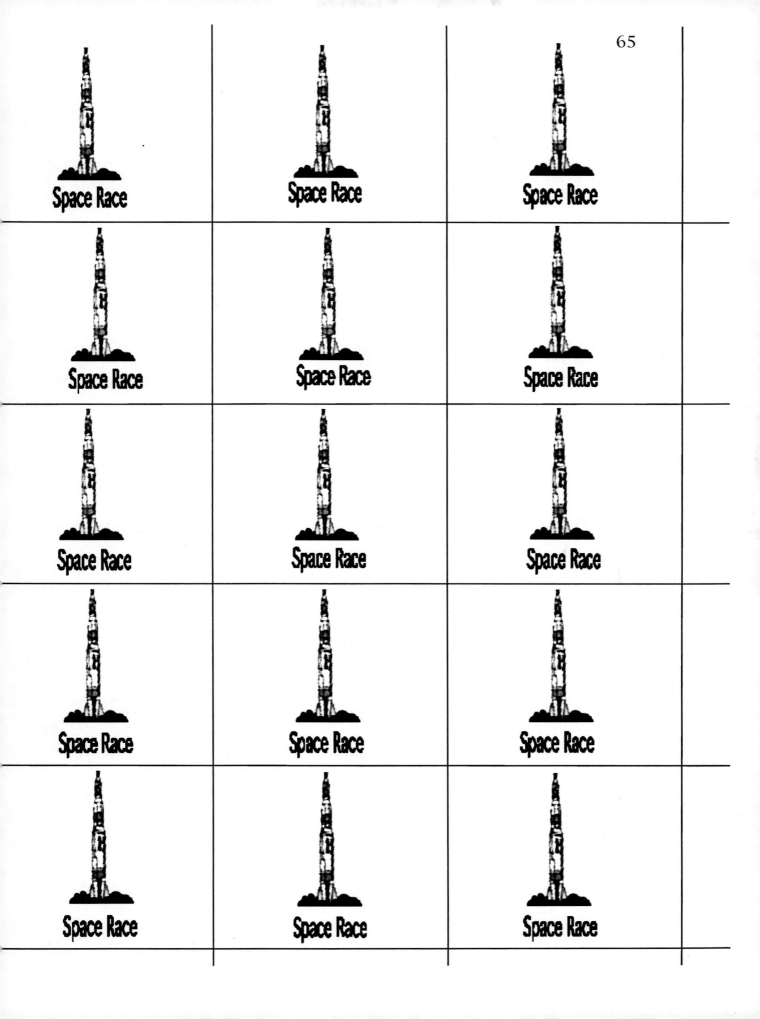

Space Race

Country: India Location: Asia Goals: economic: 5 food: 5 military: 5 Strength: 5	Country: Afghanistan Location: Asia Goals: economic: 1 food: 1 military: 1 Strength: 2	Country: Pakistan Location: Asia Goals: economic: 3 food: 1 military: 4 Strength: 4	Country: Iran Location: Asia Goals: economic: 2 food: 1 military: 4 Strength: 4	Country: Iraq Location: Middle East Goals: economic: 2 food: 1 military: 2 Strength: 3
Region: West Africa Countries: Ghana, Nigeria, Dahomey, Upper Volta, Ivory Coast, Liberia, Sierra Leone, Guinea & others Goals: economic: 5 food: 5 military: 3 Strength: 5	Region: Southeast Asia Countries: Thailand, Malaysia, Singapore & Brunei Goals: economic: 2 food: 3 military: 1 Strength: 3	Country: Israel Location: Middle East Goals: economic: 2 food: 1 military: 4 Strength: 2	Region: Arabia Countries: Saudi Arabia, Yemen, Oman, Kuwait, Bahrain, UAE & Qatar Location: Middle East Goals: economic: 1 food: 1 military: 5 Strength: 6	Region: Southern Asia Countries: Burma, Bangladesh, Nepal, & Bhut Location: Asia Goals: economic: 2 food: 4 military: 1 Strength: 3
Country: Indonesia Location: Asia Goals: economic: 4 food: 3 military: 2 Strength: 2	Region: Indochina Countries: Vietnam, Laos, & Cambodia Goals: economic: 3 food: 3 military: 3 Strength: 3	Region: Oceania Countries: Australia, New Zealand, Papua New Guinea, Fiji, Samoa & others Goals: economic: 1 food: 2 military: 2 Strength: 4	Region: The Sahara Countries: Morocco, Algeria, Tunisia, Libya, Mali, Chad, Niger, & Mauritania Goals: economic: 4 food: 4 military: 1 Strength: 3	Region: Horn Africa Countries: Sudan, Ethiopi Djibouti, & Somalia Goals: economic: 4 food: 5 military: 4 Strength: 4

Country: Philippines Location: Asia Goals: economic: 4 food: 4 military: 3 Strength: 2	Country: Taiwan Location: Asia Goals: economic: 2 food: 1 military: 5 Strength: 3	Region: Central America Countries: Guatemala, El Salvador, Honduras, Belize & Nicaragua Goals: economic: 4 food: 4 military: 4 Strength: 2	Region: The Congo Countries: Zaire, Congo, Gabon, Equatorial Guinea, Sao Tome & Principe, Cameroon, & Central Afr. Rep. Goals: economic: 5 food: 4 military: 4 Strength: 3	Country: Egypt Location: Africa Goals: economic: 3 food: 1 military: 5 Strength: 5
Country: Sweden Location: Europe Goals: economic: 1 food: 0 military: 1 Strength: 3	Country: Finland Location: Europe Goals: economic: 1 food: 0 military: 1 Strength: 2	Country: Yugoslavia Location: Europe Goals: economic: 3 food: 1 military: 3 Strength: 2	Country: Spain Location: Europe Goals: economic: 2 food: 0 military: 1 Strength: 2	Country: Portugal Location: Europe Goals: economic: 1 food: 0 military: 2 Strength: 2
Country: Mexico Location: Central America Goals: economic: 5 food: 1 military: 1 Strength: 2	Country: Panama Location: Central America Goals: economic: 3 food: 1 military: 3 Strength: 1	Country: Cuba Location: Caribbean Goals: economic: 4 food:1 military: 3 Strength: 2	Country: Colombia Location: South America Goals: economic: 3 food: 1 military: 2 Strength: 2	Country: Chile Location: South America Goals: economic: 3 food: 1 military: 2 Strength: 3

Region: Northern South America Countries: Venezuela, Surinam, Guyana Goals: economic: 3 food: 3 military: 1 Strength: 4	Region: Southern Africa Countries: South Africa, Zambia, Mozambique, Rhodesia, Lesotho, & Swaziland Goals: economic: 3 food: 2 military: 4 Strength: 4	Region: Eastern Africa Countries: Madagascar, Tanzania, Kenya, Mozambique, Malawi, Rwanda, & Burundi Goals: economic: 4 food: 4 military: 4 Strength: 3	Region: Caribbean Countries: Haiti, Dominican Republic, Bahamas, Jamaica & others Location: Caribbean Goals: economic: 4 food: 4 military: 1 Strength: 3	Region: The Levant Countries: Lebanon, Jordan, & Syri Goals: economic: 3 food: 1 military: 4 Strength: 6
Country: Paraguay Location: South America Goals: economic: 1 food: 1 military: 1 Strength: 1	Country: Brazil Location: South America Goals: economic: 4 food: 1 military: 2 Strength: 4	Country: Ecuador Location: South America Goals: economic: 1 food: 1 military: 1 Strength: 1	Country: Peru Location: South America Goals: economic: 2 food: 2 military: 2 Strength: 2	Country: Boliv Location: Sout America Goals: economic: 1 food: 1 military: 2 Strength: 2
Country: Argentina Location: South America Goals: economic: 2 food: 2 military: 3 Strength: 3	Country: Uruguay Location: South America Goals: economic: 1 food: 1 military: 1 Strength: 1	Country: China Location: East Asia Goals: economic: 5 food: 6 military: 5 Strength: 10		

Cuban Missile Crisis Simulation Teacher's Guide

Objective: To understand the intense bargaining that was necessary to avoid a nuclear catastrophe during the Cuban Missile Crisis.

Duration: 1-2 class periods.

Materials: A copy of the rules for each student. At least one copy of the country description sheet for each group. A large number of tokens in three types representing the pieces for, escalation, de-escalation, and compromise.

Procedure:

1. Sides may be chosen in whatever way the teacher chooses, but it is usually better to give them out at random. The Cuban group should be the smallest since they have the least input in the decision-making process.

2. Go over the rules with the students.

3. Students read their country's description sheet and plan their strategy for resolving the crisis.

4. The team picks one of the three cards they will play that turn.

5. The teacher determines and announces the results of any actions taken.

6. Conduct negotiations as necessary.

7. The teacher awards prestige points to any country that earned them and records the current score for each team on the board.

8. The game continues with as many rounds as necessary to determine a winner. Start each team with 10 prestige points and the first to reach 20 points is the winner.

9. Debrief.

Teacher Recommendations:

1. Carefully read the options charts for each nation in advance. Be prepared to define the terms contained in them such as air strike, ABM's, retaliation, etc.
2. Separate the groups far enough apart so that they may discuss their policy options in private. The Cubans may or may not choose to sit near the Soviets.
3. Remind students not to discuss diplomacy with the opposite side unless they have played a compromise card first, otherwise the simulation may degenerate into the two groups shouting at each other across the room or only a few active students participating while others idle. Insist that all moves be discussed by the entire group and that only one policy card may be turned in per turn: escalation, de-escalation, or compromise. Do not reveal the teams' choices until you have received the card from both teams.
4. In order to resolve any conflicts that may arise from the escalation options, the teacher should estimate a percentage chance of success depending on the complexity of the action taken. To determine success roll percentile dice (available in most game stores). If the number rolled is less than or equal to the number listed the endeavor is successful. For a slightly more difficult version of this game do not reveal the percentages to the students in advance! If you cannot find percentile dice, any reasonable element of chance such as drawing an ace from a deck of cards may be substituted. Simply adjust the probability in relation to what you believe are the option's chances of success.
5. The teacher may have to do a bit of role-playing to represent other nations that get dragged into the conflict such as Turkey or Panama.

These roles may also be assigned to a student if desired. The ramifications of some of the options may have to be invented by the teacher and explained to the students. For example, what would you tell your students might happen if they decided to blockade the Panama Canal or assassinate Castro? Have fun with it; this is the beauty of an open-ended simulation. It leads to a great discussion of "what if...?" questions in the debriefing.

6. Continue the simulation until there is a clear victor and then move on to the debriefing.

Debriefing:

1. How did it feel to come so close to the brink of disaster? How do think it felt for the leaders of the time? Why did they ever let the situation get so bad in the first place?

2. Which country had the advantage at the beginning of the game? Why?

3. In the long run which was better escalation, de-escalation, or compromise? Why?

4. What did you do well? What do you wish you had done differently?

5. How did the simulation compare to the real Cuban Missile Crisis? How would the world be different today if the crisis had been resolved the way you resolved it?

Cuban Missile Crisis Simulation

Teams: The Americans, the Soviets, and the Cubans

The Crisis: It is October of 1962 and The Soviet Union has decided to place intermediate range ballistic missiles in Cuba, only 90 miles from American shores. This act could quite possibly lead to the start of a nuclear war between the Superpowers, possibly even leading to the end of the world.

The Goal: To try and end this crisis peacefully without starting WWIII. Don't worry, if you fail, it could only mean the end of your job, your country's honor, or civilization as we know it. No pressure.

How the Game is played: each team is given a stack of option cards to demonstrate how they will deal with the crisis. The cards come in three kinds: escalation, de-escalation, and compromise. The Americans start each round followed by the Soviets, and then the Cubans. After each team plays its card the following teams meet to discuss their options and then produce the next card. A prestige point is earned each time an opponent deescalates or proposes a compromise. The winner is the team with the most prestige points.

Character descriptions:

The Soviets: You are Nikita Kruschev and the Politburo. You have been behind in the arms race. The US has recently placed missiles very close to home in Turkey, so you decided to place missiles in Cuba to threaten the US. Sure, that was a provocative move, but they started it. The Americans' recently failed in their attempt to invade the Bay of Pigs. You feel that you must protect your communist ally Fidel Castro by making sure that Cuba is never again invaded. You have assured the Americans that these missiles are there for purely defensive reasons, and can't understand why they are so surprised or upset. You never really wanted a showdown with the US, but you can't back down now without losing face. Nothing must come in the way of your goal of worldwide communism. You must rescue the innocent people of Cuba from domination by the capitalistic, imperialistic Americans!
The options:

Soviet escalations:

1. Make a televised speech denouncing American intervention in Cuba's internal affairs.
2. Accuse the US of spying and upsetting the balance of power.
3. Call up Kennedy and chew him out.
4. Publicly denounce Kennedy as an aggressor.
5. Attempt to run the blockade of ships from Cuba.
6. Intercept all ships attempting to blockade Cuba. Roll a percentile die to see how many are intercepted.
7. File a formal protest in the United Nations and demand that the US stay out of Cuba.
8. Respond to air strikes with fighter pilots or ABM's.
9. Increase the number of ships in the Caribbean.
10. Increase the number of missiles in Cuba.
11. Increase the number of missile technicians in Cuba.

12. Increase the number of ABM's in Cuba.
13. Close the US Embassy and expel its ambassadors.
14. Ask the Politburo to declare war on America.
15. Conduct an air strike on the US.
16. Engage the American fleet in battle.
17. Patrol the American coastline with subs and ships.
18. Blockade the Panama Canal.
19. Invade the Panama Canal Zone.
20. Blockade Berlin.
21. Invade South Korea.
22. Try to assassinate Kennedy.
23. Conduct an air strike on US missiles in Turkey.
24. Send Soviet troops to defend Cuba.
25. Increase aid to Communist insurrectionists in other Latin American countries.
26. Put your missiles on full alert.
27. Conduct a pre-emptive missile strike on the US.

USSR de-escalations: A reversal of any of the above escalations when possible

Soviet compromises:

1. Do nothing and hope the problem goes away.
2. Make a televised speech announcing your peaceful intentions towards America and call for an immediate resolution to the crisis.
3. Send a special envoy to Kennedy to secretly discuss terms.
4. Call for a summit meeting with Kennedy.
5. Withdraw ships to areas outside the naval blockade zone around Cuba.
6. Decrease the number of missile technicians in Cuba.
7. Decrease the number of ABM's in Cuba.
8. Remove our missiles in Cuba unilaterally.
9. Remove our missiles in Cuba only if they remove their missiles from Turkey.
10. Make a deal with Castro separately to remove the missiles but replace them with some other defensive weapons system.
11. Pledge not to place nuclear forces in Cuba ever again.
12. Propose a nuclear arms reduction treaty.

The Americans: You are John F. Kennedy and his Cabinet. You are ahead in the arms race, but fear that the Commies are catching up. The previous President placed missiles in Turkey, and you meant to remove them, but never got around to it. You are shocked that the USSR placed missiles in Cuba. You have tried to not appear soft on Communism, but have not done well in recent meetings with Kruschev. That guy must be some kind of kook! Is he out of his mind trying to start World War III? Is he just trying to embarrass the President with some kind of showdown? This is a threat to every man, woman, and child in the US! The Soviets have assured you that these missiles are there for purely defensive reasons, but you can't trust those lying Reds. You don't really want a showdown with the USSR, but you can't back down now without losing face. You are the leaders of the Free World. Nothing must come in the way of your goal of containing communism. You must protect the innocent people of the United States from annihilation by the cruel, Godless Communists!

The options:

USA escalations:

1. Reveal that you know about the exact number and location of the missiles to embarrass the Soviets.
2. Declare a national emergency and prepare for attack.
3. Blockade all ships from Cuba.
4. Blockade only military ships from Cuba.
5. Blockade only fuel tankers from Cuba.
6. Bomb Cuba with conventional bombs hitting only airfields and defenses.
7. Bomb Cuba with conventional bombs hitting only the missiles. Roll a percentile die to see how many are destroyed.
8. File a formal protest in the United Nations and demand weapons inspections of Cuba.
9. Make a televised speech denouncing the placement of the missiles.

10. Go before the OAS and ask for measures to be taken to punish Castro.

11. Go before the OAS and ask for measures for mutual defense.

12. Drop leaflets over the missile sites in Cuba warning the Soviets of an imminent US attack if the missiles are not pulled out.

13. Call up Kruschev and chew him out.

14. Publicly denounce Kruschev as an aggressor.

15. Put your missiles on full alert.

16. Ask Congress to declare war on Cuba.

17. Try to assassinate Castro.

18. Activate air defenses and continuously patrol your borders for incoming missiles.

19. Close the Soviet Embassy and expel its ambassadors.

20. Impose trade sanctions on the USSR.

21. Invade Cuba and try to overthrow Castro.

22. Engage the Soviet fleet in battle.

23. Launch a conventional invasion of the USSR.

24. Launch a nuclear strike against the USSR.

25. Threaten to retaliate against a missile strike against any Latin American country

USA de-escalations: A reversal of any of the above escalations when possible

USA compromises:

1. Do nothing and hope the problem goes away.
2. Make a televised speech announcing your peaceful intentions towards the USSR and call for an immediate resolution to the crisis.
3. Send a special envoy to Kruschev to secretly discuss terms.
4. Call for a summit meeting with Kruschev.
5. Remove our missiles in Turkey unilaterally.
6. Remove our missiles in Turkey only if they remove their missiles from Cuba.
7. Make a deal with Castro separately to remove the missiles.
8. Pledge not to invade Cuba ever again.
9. Extend diplomatic recognition to Cuba.
10. Lift the trade embargo with Cuba.
11. Return Guantanamo Bay to Cuba.
12. Propose a nuclear arms reduction treaty

The Cubans: You are Fidel Castro and the leaders of the People's Party. You have very few weapons to protect your country from the huge aggressor to the North, the USA. The US has refused to recognize your government and has cut off your trade, so you decided to make friends with the Soviets to annoy the US. Sure, that was a provocative move, but they started it. The Americans' recently failed in their attempt to invade the Bay of Pigs. You feel that you must make sure that Cuba is never again invaded. You are very proud to have Soviet missiles on your soil because it will cement the relations between your two great nations. Now that you have the same toys as the big boys, let's see if the Yankees mess with you. You have assured the Americans that these missiles are there for purely defensive reasons, and can't understand why they are so surprised or upset. You never really wanted a showdown with the US, but you can't back down now without losing face. Nothing must come in the way of your goal of worldwide communism. You must rescue the innocent people of Cuba from domination by the capitalistic, imperialistic Americans!

The options: You may not initiate any major policy options of your own. You may talk to either the Americans or the Soviets separately or together. Naturally you will lean towards what the Soviets want and they have the ultimate say in what the final decision will be for each turn. Remember that you blame America for all of the world's problems, but overall you will do what is best for Cuba, even if that means making a compromise or abandoning the Soviet alliance. You win in any situation that results in Cuba not being invaded or taken over. The stronger a pledge you can obtain to secure Cuba's freedom from American invasion, the more successful you have been.

Escalation

Escalation

Escalation

Escalation

Escalation

Escalation

Escalation

Escalation

Escalation

Escalation

Escalation

Escalation

Escalation

Escalation

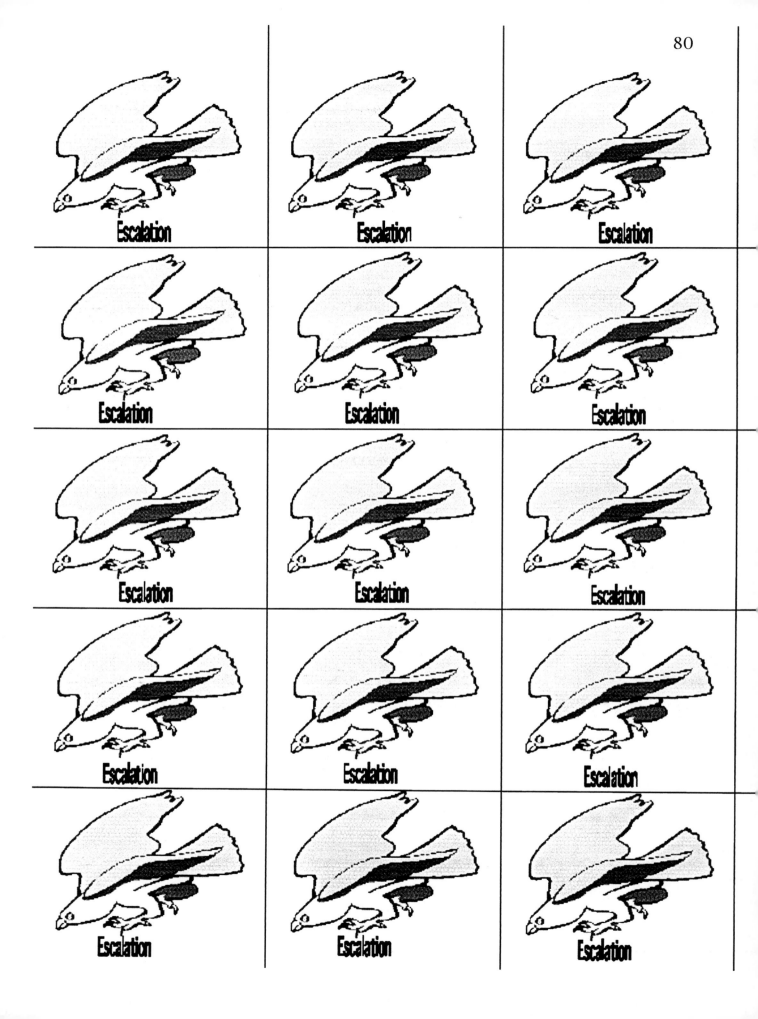

Escalation

De-escalation

De-escalation

De-escalation

De-escalation

De-escalation

De-escalation

De-escalation

De-escalation

De-escalation

De-escalation

De-escalation

De-escalation

De-escalation

De-escalation

De-escalation

Compromise

Compromise

Compromise

Compromise

Compromise

Compromise

Compromise

Compromise

Compromise

Compromise

Compromise

Compromise

Compromise

Compromise

Compromise

Hippie Day Teacher's Guide

Objective: Students will be able to get a feel for what life was like in the Sixties, answer a few questions, and bring up issues like generational conflict, pop culture and reform movements in a very unconventional way.

Duration: 1 class period.

Materials: Student-created costumes, posters, artwork, news clips, and music from the 1960's.

Procedure:
1. Preparation: Announce to the students that on a date one week from now there will be our annual Hippie Day. Students are encouraged to come in costume as much as possible. Explain to the students the guidelines for dressing "cool", and explain how to acquire costume items from their parents, thrift stores, and theater departments. Make sure your costume is a surprise to build excitement for the big, upcoming event.
2. Come early to school on Hippie Day and decorate the room with appropriate 60's posters, slogans, etc. Push the chairs back and tell students to sit on the floor. Students will notice that things are not as they normally are immediately and will be taken aback by it. Tell them to "Let it all hang out" and "get with the groove" i.e., play along with it, you will catch on soon. As students come into the room make appropriate comments about their costumes like "far out" , "groovy" and "out of sight!"

Classroom Activities:
Play a movie with scenes from the 60's with the sound turned down. Provide your own narration, reflections, and personal remembrances. Play 60's music and discuss how much impact music had on the youth culture. Explain the generation gap created by music and the Vietnam War, the history of rock and roll from underground to mainstream music, and the role of fashion in defining a generation. Compare what was viewed as shocking and rebellious in the 60's to today. Which slang words are still popular today? Finally discuss their own families role in the sixties. Were their parents hippies, were you, would your students be hippies if they had lived in the sixties?

Teacher Recommendations:

1. Hippie Day can be a refreshing break from end-of-the-year pressures. It has a deliberately "kicked-back" style in the manner of the Hippies, and setting the proper mood is everything. The object of the simulation is to make the students feel that they have stepped back in time to the 60's for a day by experiencing its sights and sounds.

2. Informality is the rule of the day. These discussions should be done informally in 60's "rap session" style. If students don't want to participate discuss nonconformism and individuality in the ethics of the Youth movement. For today only let the students "do their own thing".

3. The loose structure of the activity goes with the style of education college reformers were pushing for in those days. Don't worry, students will be having so much fun, they won't get out of control. They will be learning even though they think it is a "kick back" day.

4. Inevitably this activity will lead to some jokes about the drug culture. Do not be alarmed. Explain that drugs are definitely <u>not</u> OK, and that different people expressed their nonconformism in different ways in the 60's. Many people, even older ones, expressed sympathy for the ideals of the 60's, but did not take part in the wild extremes of the movement like drugs, nudist camps and radical politics. Many Middle Class youth remained "fashion hippies" or "Jesus People" who challenged society's injustices in milder ways.

Debriefing:

Talk about the legacy of the 60's. Have students list the various reform movements like Civil Rights, Gay Lib, Brown Power, Red Power, The Women's Movement, Ecology, and school reform. Which of these had the most lasting impact? Which movements are gaining momentum and which ones are pretty much spent? Why? What are today's reform movements? What tactics do they borrow from the protesters of the 60's? In what ways was the Vietnam War a watershed for this country?

20th Century Slang

Teacher's Guide

Objective: This is a fun activity that shows how language changes over time.

Duration: 1class period.

Materials: Hand out a copy of the 20th Century Slang handout and answer sheet to everyone.

Procedure:

1. Choose partners for the students or let them pick their own.

2. The teacher should read over the words for each decade to model the pronunciation and intonation of the terms.

3. The students look over the list of words and fill in the appropriate words for each decade on the answer sheet.

4. Debrief.

Teacher Recommendations:

1. While this is a fun activity, a word of caution should be given to students about resorting to vulgar terms when completing this activity. Because of the role of slang as a kind of code for the "inside" group, it often contains vulgarity, but try to keep it under control.

2. For further resources on historical slang consult such books as *I Hear America Talking* or *Listening to America* by Stuart Berg Flexner or *The Oxford Dictionary of Slang*. Most other slang dictionaries only give you the definition of current slang words, assuming that you already know the word. If you don't know the word, these books are the best for researching what the slang word was in the past.

Debriefing:

1. Why are there so many different ways to say the same thing? Why does slang change so often?

2. What words do you use today that are actually just old slang that has made a comeback? Were you surprised at how far back some of these terms go?

3. Where does slang come from? How do new words get started? What purpose does it serve?

4. What forces influence slang words? What do you think the slang will be like in the future?

20th Century Slang

Directions: Working with a partner, look at the following sample paragraph and substitute the underlined word with the appropriate word from each decade's word list below. Feel free to change the punctuation, form of the words or add words to make the sentences work grammatically.

Sample paragraph:
<u>Hello</u>, my name is John. I have been told that I am <u>a fairly attractive man</u>, but I have been unable to <u>get a date</u> because I don't have <u>enough money</u>. I know a <u>very beautiful girl</u> from my neighborhood, but she <u>doesn't seem to be interested in me</u>.

Hello:
1900's: What's up?
1910's: How's tricks?
1920's: Hiya kiddo!
1930's: Hello Joe, What-a-ya know?
1940's: What's cooking?
1950's: Been a while, crocodile.
1960's: What's happenin' man?
1970's: Hey man, peace!
1980's: Dude.
1990's: Whazzup?

Good looking man:
1900's: he-man
1910's: daddy
1920's: cute guy, sheik, Jazz bo, tall, dark, and handsome
1930's: smooth apple, boy-next-door
1940's: Mr. Right, glamour boy

1950's: neat, peachy keen, dream boat

1960's: cool dude, boss

1970's: hunk, stud, fox

1980's: babe

1990's: prince

Getting a date:

1900's: go courting

1910's: to get a date

1920's: go cut a rug

1930's: make time with girls

1940's: do the town, paint the town

1950's: go cruising with

1960's: take someone out

1970's: get down with someone

1980's: get some action

1990's: get hooked up with

Money:

1900's: greens

1910's: scratch

1920's: lettuce

1930's: potatoes

1940's: dough, moola

1950's: clams

1960's: bread

1970's: big bucks

1980's: denaro

1990's: bank

Very beautiful girl:

1900's: peach, a real looker

1910's: cutie

1920's: an "it" girl, girl who's the cat's meow

1930's: dream, a real dish

1940's: dollface, sweater girl, poster girl

1950's: sex symbol, knockout

1960's: groovy chick, really fab

1970's: foxy mama, fine

1980's: fresh babe

1990's: girl dat's da bomb, phat chick

Doesn't seem to be interested:

1900's: must have decided I'm in bad with her

1910's: doesn't have time for me

1920's: told me "nerts"!

1930's: said I'm not her cup of tea

1940's: couldn't care less

1950's: doesn't think I'm keen

1960's: doesn't dig me

1970's: just isn't into me

1980's: doesn't have a thing for me

1990's: doesn't think I'm all that

20th Century Slang Answer Sheet

1900's

_______________________, my name is John. I have been told that I a

_______________________, but I have been unable to _______________

_________________ because I don't have _______________________

I know a ___________________________ from my neighborhood, but

_________________________________.

1910's

_______________________, my name is John. I have been told that I a

_______________________, but I have been unable to _______________

_________________ because I don't have _______________________

I know a ___________________________ from my neighborhood, but

_________________________________.

1920's:

_______________________, my name is John. I have been told that I a

_______________________, but I have been unable to _______________

_________________ because I don't have _______________________

I know a ___________________________ from my neighborhood, but

_________________________________.

1930's

_______________________, my name is John. I have been told that I a

_______________________, but I have been unable to _______________

_________________ because I don't have _______________________

I know a ___________________________ from my neighborhood, but

_________________________________.

1940's

______________________, my name is John. I have been told that I am a ______________________, but I have been unable to ______________ ________________ because I don't have ______________________. I know a ______________________ from my neighborhood, but she ______________________.

1950's

______________________, my name is John. I have been told that I am a ______________________, but I have been unable to ______________ ________________ because I don't have ______________________. I know a ______________________ from my neighborhood, but she ______________________.

1960's

______________________, my name is John. I have been told that I am a ______________________, but I have been unable to ______________ ________________ because I don't have ______________________. I know a ______________________ from my neighborhood, but she ______________________.

1970's

______________________, my name is John. I have been told that I am a ______________________, but I have been unable to ______________ ________________ because I don't have ______________________. I know a ______________________ from my neighborhood, but she ______________________.

1980's

_____________________________, my name is John. I have been told that I a

____________________________, but I have been unable to _________________

_______________________ because I don't have ___________________________

I know a ____________________________________ from my neighborhood, but

____.

1990's

_____________________________, my name is John. I have been told that I a

____________________________, but I have been unable to _________________

_______________________ because I don't have ___________________________

I know a ____________________________________ from my neighborhood, but

____.

Today

_____________________________, my name is John. I have been told that I a

____________________________, but I have been unable to _________________

_______________________ because I don't have ___________________________

I know a ____________________________________ from my neighborhood, but

____.

US History Counterfactuals: "What if...?"

Objective: These are series of interesting critical thinking questions that encourage students to think about the possibilities of alternative outcomes in history and their consequences.

Duration: A few minutes-1 class period.

Materials: Write the question(s) for the day on the board or print them onto an overhead transparency.

Procedure:

These questions may be used to evoke student participation during a lecture, begin a class discussion or debate, or as a writing prompt for journal writing or essays.

Teacher Recommendations:

There is a really fun Internet newsgroup called "soc.history.what-if" where learned scholars and history buffs alike post messages endlessly about all kinds of speculative and alternative historical outcomes. For those who don't know what a newsgroup is, it is an electronic message board that is accessible through most Internet providers. If you can't find it on your Internet provider software, read the documentation that came with it or ask them for help. You are usually given the option to read the newsgroup or subscribe to it. If you are only visiting, choose "read messages" if you plan to go back again and again choose subscribe to newsgroup. Keep in mind that it is not a chat group, so don't expect any instant responses to your question. You must go back and check periodically to see if anyone wrote an answer to your question. After a certain period of time, old messages are deleted, so don't wait too long. Try it out some time with your classes; it really can be a great discussion starter or writing prompt. As with any Internet newsgroup, caution your students that they may come across the occasional loony out there in cyberspace, but since the group is well-moderated they usually get ridiculed by the more responsible members and quickly drop out. The only other word of caution is that if a student asks a question which has come up many times before, they may get teased as being a “newbie”. Usually the best thing to do is apologize, admit you are new, and then ask the group to respond anyway. It is always a good idea to read the Frequently Asked Questions (FAQ’s) for a newsgroup to avoid doing something that will embarrass you or annoy people.

Debriefing:

1. Ask students to create follow up questions of their own.
2. Write an essay or journal entry on their own follow up questions.
3. Post your questions on the soc.history.what-if newsgroup to see what kinds of responses your class gets.

The Pre-Columbian Era

1. What if the horse had not become extinct in North America?
2. What if ancient Americans had discovered metallurgy?
3. What if ancient Americans had discovered the wheel?
4. What if ancient Americans had sent explorers to Europe or Asia?
5. What if ancient Americans had developed nation states?
6. What if the Vikings had stayed in America?
7. What if the Vikings had told other Europeans about America?
8. What if the Chinese had sent explorers to America?
9. What if ancient Americans had stayed in Asia?
10. What if more Native Americans had been city builders?

The Age of Exploration

1. What if the Italian explorers had made their land claims for their own countries?
2. What if Amerigo Vespucci had succeeded in reaching the Pacific Ocean first?
3. What if Amerigo Vespucci had not claimed that America was part of a new world? What if he believed it was part of Asia as Columbus insisted?
4. What if Cortes had not conquered the Aztecs?
5. What if the Spanish had discovered gold in California?
6. What if Columbus had given up?
7. What if Columbus had been turned down by the Spanish?
8. What if Columbus had convinced the Portuguese to back his voyages of exploration?
9. What if Columbus had reached Asia?
10. What if Columbus had known he wasn't in Asia?
11. What if Magellan had lived to return to Spain?
12. What if Giovanni Caboto (John Cabot) had survived his second voyage?
13. What if the English or French had never claimed colonies in the New World?
14. What if the Native Americans had had resistance to European diseases?
15. What if the potato had not been discovered in the New World?
16. What if maize had not been discovered in the New World?
17. What if the French or Spanish had conquered all of North America?
18. What if Sir Francis Drake had been captured by the Spanish and hanged for piracy?
19. What if there had been no slavery in America?
20. What if tobacco never existed?
21. What if the New World never existed?
22. What if gunpowder had never been introduced to Europe?
23. What if the caravel had not been invented?
24. What if the compass had not been invented?

The Colonial Era

1. What if the Mayflower had sunk?
2. What if the Mayflower had reached its original destination?
3. What if the Mayflower had landed in South America?
4. What if the Pilgrims had stayed in England?
5. What if Pocahontas had not died of smallpox after travelling to England?
6. What if Squanto had kept his gardening tips to himself?
7. What if Bacon's Rebellion had succeeded?
8. What if all the colonists got along with the Indians as well as Miles Standish did?
9. What if the Salem Witch Trials had spread to other colonies?
10. What if the Salem Witch Trials were conducted today?
11. What if the Great Awakening had not occurred?
12. What if the colonies had not completely come under British control?
13. What if slavery had spread to the northern colonies?
14. What if all of the colonies had developed their own forms of representative government?
15. What if the British had allowed settlement beyond the Appalachian Mountains?
16. What if the Dutch had stayed in North America?
17. What if all of the Indians were on the French side in the French and Indian War?
18. What if the French had won the French and Indian War?
19. What if all of the colonies had fully industrialized?
20. What if George Washington had not fought on the British side in the French and Indian War?

The American Revolution

1. What if the works of the philosophes had been successfully repressed in the Colonies?
2. What if the Revolutionary War had been fought entirely by militia?
3. What if the Continental Army had used the tactics of the British?
4. What if the perpetrators of the Boston Tea Party had been caught?
5. What if the Bostonians had fired back at the British during the Boston Massacre?
6. What if Paul Revere had chickened out and stayed in bed that night?
7. What if the Continental Army had conquered Canada?
8. What if the colonies had peacefully settled their differences with England and remained British?
9. What if the British had permanently lowered taxes in the colonies?
10. What if the British had permitted colonists to stand for election in the British Parliament?
11. What if a different king had been on the throne of England during the Revolutionary War?

The American Revolution (continued)

12. What if the British had won the Revolutionary War? What impact would this have had on America and on future revolutions?
13. What if the French Revolution had occurred before the American Revolution?
14. What if the French had not aided the Americans in their Revolution?
15. What if the Patriots had been communist?
16. What if George Washington had declined to lead the Continental Army?
17. What if Benedict Arnold had remained loyal to the American cause in the Revolutionary War?
18. What if there had been no Tories in the Revolutionary War?
19. What if George Washington had become a dictator?
20. What if George Washington had become the king of America?
21. What if the Declaration of Independence was written by someone else?
22. What if the Declaration of Independence was written earlier?
23. What if the Declaration of Independence was written later?
24. What if the Declaration of Independence was signed by only some of the colonies?
25. What if Cornwallis had refused to surrender?
26. What if Thomas Jefferson or Benjamin Franklin had helped to write the Constitution?
27. What if the Articles of Confederation were still in effect?
28. What if the Bill of Rights had not been passed?

The Early Republic

1. What if the Whiskey Rebellion had succeeded?
2. What if John Marshall's assertion of the principal of judicial review had been rejected by Congress or the President?
3. What if Thomas Jefferson had said no to the Louisiana Purchase?
4. What if Sacajawea had been a stay-at-home mom?
5. What if Lewis & Clark had found a navigable river passage to the Pacific Ocean?
6. What if the Alien & Sedition Acts were still in effect?
7. What if the Burr conspiracy had succeeded?
8. What if Aaron Burr had not killed Alexander Hamilton?
9. What if the British had successfully reconquered the United Sates during the War of 1812?
10. What if the British had not been fighting the French while fighting the United Sates during the War of 1812?
11. What if the news of the Treaty of Ghent had arrived before the Battle of New Orleans in the War of 1812?
12. What if we had fought the French during the War of 1812?
13. What if the Monroe Doctrine had actually been put to the test?
14. What if the Bank of the United States were still in operation?

The Early Republic (continued)

15. What if the Federalist Party had not died out?
16. What if the US had gone to war with Britain over Oregon?
17. What if Florida had remained Spanish?
18. What Andrew Jackson had been killed in one of his duels?
19. What Andrew Jackson had been impeached?
20. What if Andrew Jackson had honored the Supreme Courts decision to block the removal of Indians from the Southeast?
21. What if Santa Anna had been a better general or leader?
22. What if Texas had remained a separate nation?
23. What if Texas had been divided into separate states upon entering the Union?

The Mexican War

1. What if Mexico had agreed to our proposal to buy some of its territory?
2. What if Mexicans had discovered gold in California before the Mexican-American War?
3. What if Mexico had not allowed foreigners to settle on its land?
4. What if the northern provinces of Mexico had been more heavily settled before the Mexican-American War?
5. What if the Californian Mexicans had united in the defense of Mexican rule in California?
6. What if the California missions had not been sold off by the Mexican government?
7. What if the United States had decided to keep all of Mexico after its defeat in the Mexican-American War?

The California Gold Rush

1. What if the California Indians had survived the Gold Rush in large enough numbers to be placed in reservations as in other parts of the United States?
2. What if everyone who set out for California in the Gold Rush had actually survived the trip?
3. What if there were no gold in California?
4. What if the Oregon Trail and other famous Trails had proved impassible?
5. What if there had been a Panama Canal at the time of the Gold Rush?

The Antebellum Era

1. What if Eli Whitney had not invented the cotton gin?
2. What if the Missouri Compromise had remained in effect?
3. What if Nat Turner's Rebellion had succeeded?
4. What if Denmark Vesey's Rebellion had succeeded?
5. What if John Brown's Rebellion had succeeded?
6. What if the Compromise of 1850 had worked?

The Antebellum Era (continued)

7. What if the Kansas-Nebraska Act had not been passed?
8. What if Kansas had been settled by all pro-slavery or anti-slavery forces and the events which earned it the nickname "Bloody Kansas" had not occurred?
9. What if the Whig Party had not dissolved?
10. What if the Republican Party had never arisen?
11. What if Abraham Lincoln had not been elected?
12. What if the Border States had also seceded?
13. What if Abraham Lincoln had decided to let the seceding states leave in peace?
14. What if the Dred Scott case had been decided in his favor?

The Civil War

1. What if Fort Sumter had not surrendered?
2. What if Abraham Lincoln had had a competent general from the beginning of the war?
3. What if Robert E. Lee had fought for the North?
4. What if the North had surrendered after the Battle of Bull Run?
5. What if the battle of Antietam had ended the war in a draw?
6. What if Abraham Lincoln had not issued the Emancipation Proclamation?
7. What if the South had won the battle of Gettysburg?
8. What if Pickett's charge had never happened?
9. What if George Meade had pursued Lee's army after the battle of Gettysburg?
10. What if Grant had become a hopeless alcoholic?
11. What if there had been larger battles in California and other parts of the West?
12. What if England had intervened in the war on the part of the South?
13. What if the Confederacy had had a stronger economy?
14. What if the Confederacy had had more industry?
15. What if the North had also had slavery?
16. What if the North had had a stronger army from the beginning?
17. What if the Confederate capital had not been moved to Richmond?
18. What if Robert E. Lee had surrendered sooner?

Reconstruction

1. What if Abraham Lincoln had not been assassinated?
2. What if all of the other assassinations plotted for the same evening as Abraham Lincoln's had succeeded?
3. What if John Wilkes Booth had not been caught?
4. What if John Wilkes Booth had stood trial?
5. What if Andrew Johnson had been removed from office?
6. What if Grant had become president sooner?

Reconstruction (continued)

7. What if the Radical Republicans had gotten their way in their desire to punish the South after the Civil War?
8. What if greater numbers of Confederate soldiers had been imprisoned or killed after the war?
9. What if the Reconstruction amendments to the Constitution had not been passed?
10. What if the Freedman's Bureau had not been created?
11. What if all of the freed slaves had stayed in the South after the war?
12. What if the African Americans who were elected during the Reconstruction Era had remained in office for several years?
13. What if Jim Crow laws had not been passed?
14. What if the KKK had been hunted down and destroyed by the end of Reconstruction?
15. What if Southern states had rejoined the Union sooner?

Westward Expansion

1. What if the Transcontinental Railroad had never been built?
2. What if the Transcontinental Railroad had been built before or during the Civil War?
3. What if the Irish or Chinese had been unavailable to help build The Transcontinental Railroad?
4. What if the Mexicans had not shared their cowboy skills with others?
5. What if the Mormon Territory had become a separate nation?
6. What if the Indian tribes had not been granted American citizenship?
7. What if the Dawes Act had been successful in carrying out the reforms that it intended?
8. What if Chief Joseph had made it to Canada?
9. What if George Custer had won the Battle of Little BigHorn?
10. What if the Battle of Little BigHorn had not occurred?
11. What if barbed wire had not been invented?
12. What if the steel plow had not been invented?
13. What if scientific farming had not been invented?
14. What if the "Great American Desert" had really been one?
15. What if trees were more widely available throughout the Great Plains and the Southwest?
16. What if the American bison were still as numerous as they were in pre-settlement times?
17. What if the Spanish had not introduced horses or mules to the Great Plains?
18. What if the Comstock Lode had not been found?
19. What if any one of the gold or silver rushes in the West such as Colorado, the Klondike, or the Black Hills had not occurred?
20. What if gunfights had been outlawed?

Westward Expansion (continued)

21. What if Geronimo had not been captured?
22. What if Pancho Villa had been captured?

The Industrial Revolution

1. What if the Wright Brothers had stuck to building bicycles?
2. What if the Wright Brothers had crash-landed?
3. What if the refinement of petroleum had been invented 100 or 200 years earlier?
4. What if ways had been found to curb the pollution and waste of industrialism sooner?
5. What if labor laws had been introduced sooner?
6. What if there were no labor unions?
7. What if the labor union movement had been successfully repressed?
8. What if women had labor unions as powerful as those of men?
9. What if the railroad had not been invented?
10. What if the Bessemer Process had not been invented?
11. What if ways to improve the food supply had not been found?
12. What if modern medicine had not arrived to improve living conditions and extend life expectancy?
13. What if the steam engine had been invented earlier?
14. What if cheap labor from immigrants, women, children and freed slaves had been unavailable?
15. What if the Progressive Movement had never taken place?
16. What if the reforms of the Progressive Movement all been accomplished by the Progressive Party?
17. What if we were still on the silver or gold standard?
18. What if the trusts had not been busted?
19. What if the muckrakers had been censored or repressed?
20. What if the electoral reforms of the Progressive Movement had not been made?
21. What if the Clean Food and Drug Act had not been passed?
22. What if Theodore Roosevelt had not adopted some of the reforms of the progressives as his own?
23. What if a Socialist had been elected president?
24. What if America had been lacking in some of the key mineral resources that made the Industrial Revolution possible?
25. What if Thomas Edison or Alexander Graham Bell had been unable to get their inventions to work?
26. What if Henry Ford's idea had been a flop?

Imperialism

1. What if Russia had never sold Alaska to the United States?
2. What if the United States had tried to gain colonies in Africa?
3. What if the United States had tried to gain colonies on mainland Asia?
4. What if the United States had gone to war with Britain over Hawaii?

Imperialism (continued)

5. What if the Age of imperialism were still going on today? What would the American Empire look like?
6. What if Europeans had ignored the Monroe Doctrine?
7. What if Europeans had ignored the Open Door Policy?
8. What if the French had succeeded in building the Panama Canal?
9. What if the US had failed to complete the Panama Canal?
10. What if the Panamanians were not interested in independence?
11. What if the Yellow journalism prior to the Spanish-American War had been proved to be false?
12. What if Teddy Roosevelt had been killed in the Spanish-American War?
13. What if Teddy Roosevelt's plans to have the US invade Guam and the Philippines had been foiled by his superiors?
14. What if Spain had won the Spanish-American War?
15. What if it had been proved at the time that the sinking of the Maine was an accident?
16. What if most of the rest of the Latin American countries were still under Spanish control at the time of the Spanish-American War?
17. What if the conquered Spanish colonies had been given their independence right away?
18. What if another nation had decided to fire upon the Great White Fleet?
19. What if the Filipino Insurrection had succeeded?
20. What if the United States still owned all of the territories it gained in the Spanish-American War?

WWI

1. What if the Archduke Francis Ferdinand had lived?
2. What if the British had tanks at the beginning of WWI?
3. What if the Germans had used all of their battleships during the war?
4. What if Germany had only attacked France or Russia in WWI?
5. What if the Schlieffen Plan had worked?
6. What if Italy had not changed it alliances or stayed neutral?
7. What if Woodrow Wilson's attempts at mediation had succeeded?
8. What if the Russian Revolution had never happened?
9. What if Lenin had not returned to Russia?
10. What if the Russian Revolution had happened earlier?
11. What if America had stayed neutral?
12. What if the White army had won the Russian Civil War?
13. What if the Czar and his family had lived?
14. What if the Treaty of Versailles had been more lenient on the Central Powers?
15. What if the Ottoman Empire or Austro-Hungarian Empire had remained intact?
16. What if the US Senate had ratified the Treaty of Versailles?

WWI (continued)

17. What if Woodrow Wilson's health had not failed him?
18. What if Woodrow Wilson's 14 Points had worked?

The Great Depression

1. What if the stock market had not crashed?
2. What if Hoover had been re-elected?
3. What if Hoover had been able to solve the Great Depression his way?
4. What if FDR had only served one or two terms?
5. What if FDR had not declared the bank holiday?
6. What if the Dust Bowl had never happened or happened in another part of the country?
7. What if the Bonus Army had been given what they demanded?
8. What if the New Deal had been completely overturned by the Supreme Court?
9. What if none of the New Deal had been overturned by the Supreme Court?
10. What if the court-packing strategy of FDR had worked?
11. What if Huey Long had been elected president?
12. What if Huey Long's "deduct box" were found?
13. What if FDR had given up and turned to socialism or fascism?
14. What if the Depression in the US was as bad as it was in Europe?
15. What if the Depression had led to mass starvation in the US?
16. What if Bonnie & Clyde or other gangsters had not been killed?
17. What if the Depression had ended sooner?
18. What if the Depression had not ended at the outbreak of WWII?

WWII

1. What if Mussolini had stayed a Socialist?
2. What if Mussolini had stayed neutral?
3. What if Mussolini had not been allied with Hitler?
4. What if Mussolini had been a better military planner? Could the Italian armed forces have performed better?
5. What if Hitler had had a more normal family life during his upbringing?
6. What if Hitler had been successful as an artist?
7. What if Hitler had been killed during WWI?
8. What if Hitler had been replaced as leader of the Nazi Party?
9. What if Mein Kampf had been a flop?
10. What if the Beer Hall Putsch had worked?
11. What if Hitler had remained a democratic leader?
12. What if Britain and her allies had decided to stop Hitler sooner?
13. What if Hitler had honored the Munich Accords?
14. What if Hitler had not attacked Poland?
15. What if Appeasement had continued?
16. What if the Maginot Line had worked?

WWII (continued)

17. What if Dunkirk had failed?
18. What if the Axis powers had gotten control of Egypt and the Suez Canal?
19. What if Italy had surrendered sooner?
20. What if Mussolini had committed suicide?
21. What if Mussolini had successfully escaped to Germany?
22. What if Italy had not changed sides in the war?
23. What if Hitler had not attacked Russia?
24. What if Hitler had attacked Russia earlier in the summer?
25. What if Hitler had conquered Moscow?
26. What if Japan had attacked Russia instead of the US?
27. What if Stalin had not killed so many generals in the purges?
28. What if Stalin had surrendered?
29. What if the Germans had not tried to conquer Stalingrad?
30. What if the Germans had conquered the Baku oilfields?
31. What if some of the neutral countries like Spain had joined the war?
32. What if Hitler had had a better navy at the beginning of the war?
33. What if radar and sonar had not been invented?
34. What if the Germans had invented the atomic bomb first?
35. What if the assassination attempt on Hitler had worked?
36. What if the Invasion of Normandy had taken place at an earlier or later time?
37. What if the Battle of the Bulge had succeeded in pushing back the Allies?
38. What if the Americans and British had conquered all of Germany before the Russians arrived?
39. What if Hitler had not committed suicide?
40. What if Japan had concentrated all of her strength on conquering China?
41. What if Japan had conquered Australia or India?
42. What if Japan had never attacked Pearl Harbor?
43. What if the US had been prepared for the attack on Pearl Harbor?
44. What if the attack on Pearl Harbor had succeeded in sinking all of the American aircraft carriers?
45. What if the US had decided to attack Japan directly instead of island hopping?
46. What if the atomic bomb had not been used on Japan?
47. What if the atomic bomb had been used on Germany?
48. What if Japan still hadn't surrendered after the 2 atomic bombs were dropped?
49. What if the atomic bomb had been only been demonstrated, but not dropped on a city?
50. What if the atomic bomb had been used on a strictly military target?
51. What if there had been only one atomic bomb?

WWII (continued)

52. What if WWII had been resolved by means of a treaty like the Versailles Treaty following WWI with reparations, demilitarization, and loss of land from the defeated powers?

The Cold War

1. What if Roosevelt had lived to finish his fourth term in office?
2. What if there had been no atomic bomb?
3. What if the hydrogen bomb had not been invented?
4. What if the US and USSR had remained allies?
5. What if Germany had remained united and neutral?
6. What if the Soviets had invented the atomic bomb first?
7. What if the Soviets had invented the hydrogen bomb first?
8. What if the Soviets had allowed free elections in Eastern Europe after WWII?
9. What if the Nationalists had won the Civil War in China?
10. What if Korea had been completely reunified by one side or the other?
11. What if China had stayed out of Korea?
12. What if Truman had allowed MacArthur to remain as the commander of Allied forces in Korea?
13. What if the Soviets had used combat troops in Korea?
14. What if the US had used the atomic bomb in North Korea?
15. What if the UN had been involved in Vietnam the same way that they were in Korea?
16. What if the United Nations had not been formed?
17. What if NATO or the Warsaw Pact had not been formed?
18. What if the Marshall Plan had not been implemented?
19. What if Sputnik had been a flop?
20. What if the USA had launched a satellite before Sputnik?
21. What if the Berlin Blockade had succeeded?
22. What if the US had intervened to aid the revolt in Hungary against Communism?
23. What if the United States had been Communist and the Russians were Capitalists?
24. What if Joseph McCarthy was right about there being Communists in the Army and the State Department?
25. What if Nixon had been president instead of Eisenhower?
26. What if Nixon had been president instead of Kennedy?
27. What if Fidel Castro had not become a Communist?
28. What if Eisenhower had been president instead of Kennedy during the Bay of Pigs invasion?
29. What if the Bay of Pigs invasion had worked?
30. What if the CIA's attempts to kill Fidel Castro had worked?
31. What if the Cuban Missile Crisis had actually turned into a full-scale war?

The Cold War (continued)

32. What if the US had attempted to invade Cuba during the Cuban Missile Crisis?
33. What if the Soviets had used the missiles in Cuba?
34. What if Kennedy had lived to finish his term in office? Would he have escalated our involvement in Vietnam to a full-scale war?
35. What if the US had invaded North Vietnam?
36. What if the US had used nuclear missiles on North Vietnam?
37. What if the Chinese and Soviets had not aided North Vietnam?
38. What if the US had not invaded Cambodia?
39. What if there had been no Ho Chi Minh?
40. What if there had been no Ho Chi Minh Trail?
41. What if the US had withdrawn from Vietnam earlier?
42. What if the US had never been involved in Vietnam?
43. What if there were still two Vietnam's today?
44. What if both sides had honored their obligations under the Paris Cease-Fire Agreements?
45. What if the Prague Spring had succeeded?
46. What if Nixon had not gone to China?
47. What if the Great Leap Forward had worked?
48. What if the Cultural Revolution had succeeded?
49. What if China had been admitted to the United Nations earlier?
50. What if the Great Leap Forward had not occurred?
51. What if the Cultural Revolution had not occurred?
52. What if Mao had remained a Confucianist?
53. What if someone like Mao were in charge of China today?
54. What if the Tiananmen Square Revolt had succeeded?
55. What if Ronald Reagan had been president in 1976?
56. What if Jimmy Carter had succeeded in rescuing the hostages in Iran?
57. What if the SALT II Treaty had been ratified?
58. What if the Soviets had succeeded in taking over Afghanistan?
59. What if Ronald Reagan had not proposed arms control talks with Soviets?
60. What if Ronald Reagan had not been willing to negotiate with Gorbachev?
61. What if Ronald Reagan had not increased arms spending in the early 1980's?
62. What if the Strategic Defense Initiative had been completed?
63. What if Mikhail Gorbachev had remained a Stalinist style of Communist?
64. What if Mikhail Gorbachev's reforms had worked?
65. What if the USSR had not broken apart? What would the world be like today?
66. What if the USSR had won the Cold War? What would the world be like today?
67. What if Boris Yeltsin had not forced Gorbachev out of power?

The Cold War (continued)
68. What if the Communist revolt against Gorbachev had worked?
69. What if the Berlin Wall had not come down?
70. What if Gorbachev had resisted Eastern Europe's attempts to no longer be Communist?
71. What if Eastern Europe had remained Communist?
72. What if Gorbachev had resisted the Baltic State's attempts to leave the USSR?
73. What if peace in the Middle East had been achieved?
74. What if Israel's enemies had succeeded in taking it over?
75. What if Palestinian statehood had been achieved peacefully?

Recent History
1. What if the US had decided not to do anything about Iraq's invasion of Kuwait?
2. What if the Persian Gulf had not contained oil?
3. What if George Bush had not been able to assemble the coalition of allies against Iraq?
4. What if Saddam Hussein had been killed in the Gulf War?
5. What if all of Iraq had been occupied during Desert Storm?
6. What if the US had decided not to do anything about the war in the Balkans?
7. What if Slobodan Milosovic had completed his campaign of ethnic cleansing in the Balkans?
8. What if the savings and loan crisis had not led to a downturn economy at the end of George Bush's term of office?
9. What if the election had been held shortly after the conclusion of the Gulf War?
What I George Bush had not said, Read my lips... no new taxes"?
10. What if Bill Clinton had not imitated the conservative economic policies of the Republicans?
11. What if the economy had not improved under Bill Clinton's tenure?
12. What if Clinton's national health care program had been signed into law?
13. What if Paula Jones or Monica Lewinsky had kept their silence?
14. What if Bill Clinton had resigned or been removed from office?
15. What if the impeachment and trial of Bill Clinton had focused on other issues such as the allegedly illegal foreign campaign contributions or the Whitewater affair?
16. What would the legacy of the Clinton Administration been if it had been free of scandals?
17. What if Albert Gore had won the recounts that he wanted in the 2000 presidential election?
18. What if Albert Gore had not contested the election results in the 2000 presidential election?
19. What if the Supreme Court had not decided to call a halt to the recounts in the 2000 presidential election?

Recent History (continued)

20. What if George W. Bush had had adequate warning of the terrorist acts of September 11, 2001?
21. What if the terrorist acts of September 11, 2001 had not occurred and George W. Bush had been free to pursue the domestic agenda he had campaigned on?
22. What if more of the airplanes had crashed short of their targets during the terrorist acts of September 11, 2001?
23. What if the plane headed for the White House had reached its target?
24. What if George W. Bush had not decided to go to war in Afghanistan?
25. What if Osama bin Laden were killed or captured?

About the author

Richard Di Giacomo graduated from San José State University with a BA in Ancient and Medieval history, a BA in Social Science and an MA in American History. He has been a teacher for 16 years and has taught in a variety of schools from private and continuation schools to public high schools. He has taught everything from at risk and limited English students to honors and college preparatory classes. The subjects he has taught include US and World History, Government, Economics, Bible and Ethics, History of the Cold War, and Contemporary World History.

He has been a reviewer and contributor to textbooks, and a frequent presenter at social studies conferences on the use of simulations, videos, and computers in education. Rich's love for role-playing and strategy games led him to develop his unique books which combine the open-ended outcomes of role-playing with the tough decisions made by people in times of historical crisis. Students often relate that these are their most memorable and enjoyable activities of the year. They bring history to life so vividly that students can't seem to stop talking about the simulations long after class is over!

How to contact the author:

It is my sincere hope that you will find these simulations as enjoyable, educational, and easy-to-use as I have. They are really unlike any other kind of simulation available in the market today. Should you feel like you need further information or suggestions as to how to run these simulations in your classroom, please contact me by:

1. e-mail at Krinibar@AOL.COM

2. or via US Mail at:

Richard Di Giacomo

2486 Aram Avenue

San Jose, California 95128 USA

3. Or visit our new webpage at: http://www.magnificopublications.com.

Also by the same author:

Short Role-playing Simulations for World History Classrooms 3rd Edition © 2003

ISBN 0-9706237-0-4 15.95

With the following simulations:

1. Roman Emperor Simulation
2. Medieval Conversation
3. Christopher Columbus Trial
4. Martin Luther Trial
5. French Revolution Simulation
6. Taking Colonies: A World History Writing Assignment
7. Great Powers Game (W.W.I)
8. W.W.II Debates
9. Cold War Simulation
10. World History Counterfactuals: "What if...?"

and...

THE INFLUENCE OF RENAISSANCE HUMANISM ON THE EXPLORERS OF THE ITALIAN ERA OF DISCOVERY

By Richard Di Giacomo

 ISBN 09706237-2-0 15.95

Our newest release:

THE HISTORY TEACHER'S REALLY BAD JOKE BOOK

Magnifico Publications Order Form

HOW TO ORDER

(1) Order our books through our web page at http://www.magnificopublications.com.
(2) Order them through the following web pages:
Social Studies School Services. http://catalog.socialstudies.com/c/@FcDiHj_IWo0jw/Pages/list.html?nocache@8+curList@0.
Teachers' Discovery. http://www.teachersdiscovery.com.
Amazon.com. http://www.amazon.com/exec/obidos/tg/stores/detail/-/books/0970623704/reviews/qid%3D996735781/sr%3D1-2/ref%3Dsc%5Fb%5F2/104-9864913-9328725.
(5) Contact Magnifico Publications directly at 408-286-5179 or E-mail us at krinibar@aol.com.
(7) Mail this order form to: Magnifico Publications 2486 Aram Ave. San Jose, CA. 95128.

Name______________________________

School or Organization______________________________

Department: ______________________________

Address______________________________

City______________ State______________ ZIP______________

Country______________ E-Mail Address______________

Phone (______)______-______________ Ship to: ______________

ISBN:	Title(s):	# ordered	cost
ISBN 09706237-1-2	*Role-playing Simulations for US History Classrooms*		15.95
ISBN 09706237-0-4	*Role-playing Simulations for World History Classrooms*		15.95
ISBN 09706237-2-0	*The New Man and the New World: The Influence of Renaissance Humanism on the Explorers of the Italian Era of Discovery*		15.95
ISBN 09706237-3-9	*The History Teacher's Really Bad Joke Book*		8.50
		Shipping & handling	4.50
		Tax (CA only)	
		Total cost	